23596·

SACRED TONGUES

David Scott is Rector of St Lawrence and St Swithun, Winchester and Warden of the Diocesan School of Spirituality. His *Selected Poems* are published by Bloodaxe Books and his most recent book for SPCK, *An Anglo-Saxon Passion*, was published in 1999.

DEDICATION

I would like to dedicate this book, firstly to the parishioners of St Lawrence and St Swithun-upon-Kingsgate, Winchester, with thanks for their support and friendship over nine years. Then to Bishop Michael Scott-Joynt and Lou, for the use of a room in their home to complete the manuscript. Also, to my long-suffering family, for whom Andrewes and Company have become household names; and to Bishop Kenneth Stevenson and Sarah for hosting seminars where seventeenth-century spiritual matters are discussed.

In addition, I would like to thank Gill Hickson for helping with the typing; Robin Keeley for suggesting the idea in the first place; and Joanna Moriarty of SPCK, whose supportive editorial guidance has steered me through.

SACRED TONGUES

The Golden Age of Spiritual Writing

David Scott

First published in Great Britain 2001
Society for Promoting Christian Knowledge
Holy Trinity Church
Marylebone Road
London NW1 4DU

Unless otherwise indicated, biblical quotations are from
The Revised English Bible © 1989 Oxford and
Cambridge University Presses

British Library Cataloguing-in-Publication Data
A catalogue record for this book is available
from the British Library

ISBN 0–281–05221–2

Typeset by Wilmaset Ltd, Birkenhead, Wirral
Printed in Great Britain by
The Cromwell Press, Trowbridge, Wiltshire

CONTENTS

INTRODUCTION

What have we learnt from living since we started
. . . except to re-enkindle commonplace?
O house, O sloping field, O setting sun!

R. M. Rilke (1967)

What is important is the recognition of the deep worth of the
Anglican writings and of the elements of mysticism which
Anglicans themselves ignore.

Thomas Merton (Daggy, 1997)

It was an earnest school reading competition. One of the sixth
form knew I was going in for it, and suggested I read Donne's
Holy Sonnet 10, 'Death be not proud'. I read it over and over
again, and like most things learnt by heart at an impressionable
age, it has stayed with me ever since. So a book on seventeenth-
century spiritual writers will have to start there with me, in a
small room, high up in a tower, with a buff-coloured, clothy
paper, Penguin edition of John Donne's poetry.

Being a boarder at a largely day school, there was time when
most had gone home, to meet in the library with a few others
who shared an interest in poetry. We brought along a poem. I
was quite keen on trying out my Scottish accent on the poems of
Robert Burns. I had picked the book up on a recent holiday at
Pitlochry. We sat round and read these poems to each other,
and one night someone brought along the love poems of
Donne. Having only come across this poem on death, I was
fascinated to discover this other strain of Donne's poetry
which resonated hugely with the hormonal years of boarding-
school adolescence. I liked both, I have to say. Donne became
the companion of my mixed-up youthful years where religion
and infatuation went hand in hand, right up to the time of university. I reckon that if George Herbert had been read that
evening instead of the love poems of John Donne, there would
hardly have been a flicker of interest. Herbert's poems came for
me with a volcanic power at university when the specifically
religious struggle that was so much a part of Herbert's life was

1

able to vocalize my feelings exactly: 'I struck the board and cried, "No more! I will abroad!"'

Not far away from school, down the Stratford Road, was the famous theatre, and the home of the Royal Shakespeare Company. Every term at school, in the late 1950s and early 1960s, a coach would take parties of us to see the plays of Shakespeare. Donne and Shakespeare are not a bad start for a life devoted mainly to poetry and religion. We also 'did' Shakespeare productions at school, and because it was an all boys' school, I served my apprenticeship playing parts like Portia. The iambics got ingrained into me. Reading a celebration of 'Fifty Years of Shakespeare and the Stratford Theatres' I came across a recollection by Jane Lapotaire who remembered the almost sensual bliss of rolling the Shakespearian words around in her mouth, and realizing what a lucky privilege it was for her to do that for a living, for half the year, at Stratford. 'We lived on words' and the work was 'soul food', she said. That brought the seventeenth century to life for her, as if it was a living experience, 'felt along the heart', and in this case in the mouth and in the soul.

The other great literary influence of my school days was the Authorized Version of the Bible. The King James Version, as it is also called, was the staple diet of the chapel services at school, until one exciting night in Evensong in 1963, the headmaster introduced us to the New English Bible. That was only one of the shocks that punctuated our 1960s schooling. The Authorized Version was a challenge to boy readers, as Shakespeare plays must have been to boy Portias, and boy Juliets, in the Globe Theatre. When I was reading it in public I remember a crucial inversion from 1 Kings, where I should have read Saul was a 'just man' and it came out 'just a man', and a friend of mine had great difficulty with '"e that 'ath hears to 'ear'.

I do not lament the revolution into modern English of the Bible: there is so much more to the Bible than its poetry and the sound of the English words. There is the gospel itself, the meaning, the presence of God through and through, but the language of the seventeenth century, Shakespeare, Donne, and the Authorized Version has a life and a sinew which is itself theological or, as this book tries to convey, spiritual. It says something about God by the way in which sense and sound are intertwined.

The first, everyday mystery to grapple with is how language can convey truth. Over and over again I find myself confronted by this mystery: how sounds strung together can be both a token of meaning and a meaning in themselves. How saying a word brings what that word represents alive. How in saying 'God', God is given life. To say 'love' in a particular context is to bring love into existence. This is one of the everyday mysteries of words. They are such simple things, and yet they open up worlds, and they change lives.

There are probably very good reasons why the language of the seventeenth century was so robust, physical, and extensive. I came to its power simply by reading it, hearing it, tasting it in the mouth when speaking it, feeling it hit nerves all round the body, sensing that it was forming values and ideas in my mind. I came at it experientially, and therefore am short of historical and linguistic reasons as to why it was so powerful and beautiful at the same time. It was largely a case of 'O, taste and see'. The language will be one of the main characters in this book, but not, I feel I have to apologize, in academic dress.

The book deals with writers, and obviously writers traffic in words, and printed words live on. The thoughts of the hearts of believers who attended churches in the seventeenth century are mainly lost. One way of coming at this underworld of unspoken attitudes is sideways by listening between the lines of Herbert's great prose work, *A Priest to the Temple or, The Country Parson His Character etc.* Publication gives a particular sort of worldly immortality, which many who felt strongly about spiritual things at the time will not receive in our own day.

The influence of Magdalen Herbert on her son George, and on John Donne as well, is recorded, but we do not, unfortunately, have her side of the correspondence. We do have a letter from George Herbert to his mother, in which he describes how he intends to devote himself to religious, rather than secular, poetry, and he does that largely through the influence of his mother. She might have been the more spiritual person. Inevitably language, words, written words provide our main window into the past when it comes to spiritual writers.

History has a bad press with the young of today. Why worry

about the past when the present has so much to be concerned with? For my generation, T. S. Eliot has been very influential in helping us to see history as a present, and not only a past, reality. We owe much of our interest in the seventeenth century to him, which comes to us through his essays and his poetry, particularly in the *Four Quartets*, and more recently through the publication of his Clark Lectures of the 1920s. It is in that wonderful poetic insight into the spirituality of the period that we see how religious history is never locked into the past, but it is of the 'now'. 'History', Eliot wrote, 'is now.'

Spiritual writing

There is often an instant reaction to the words 'spiritual' or 'spirituality' which evokes a sense of the strange, the unusual, the hidden, the esoteric, and we might well ask what this has got to do with a God who through history has longed to reveal himself. What has this got to do with the God who delights to reveal himself to the childlike and the simple? The essence of spirituality I wish to deal with here, is not in the arcane and complicated systems that many religions have developed alongside their mainstream beliefs, but is a way of looking at God and the world. It involves some things about which you might say, 'Oh, I've been feeling that all my life.' For others, it might spark off new ways of thinking and experiencing. Spirituality is to do with the surprise of seeing new things. It is about concentrating on the things of this world until new patterns are discovered which speak of eternity, and it is about the nature of things which inspire a choice for goodness, kindness, and gentleness in our dealings with others. It is about looking at something as simple as bread, and seeing how it is transformed into the body of Christ, through our faith and commitment to the example of the life of Jesus.

The spirituality of these writers is to do with seeing the extraordinary in the ordinary, and the classic text is Herbert's poem 'The Elixir', perhaps more familiar to us as the hymn, 'Teach me, my God and King'. This poem encourages us to offer up our daily tasks as a means of 'seeing' the purposes of God and, by that initial act of seeing, to go even further and discover how that can change the nature of the tasks themselves, from grind

4

to grace. How these two great realities, heaven and earth, come together, and the point at which they come together interests me, and it interested the writers of the seventeenth century. Perhaps it has been of perpetual fascination how the ordinary, accessible things of daily life, such as words, bodies, bread, wine, things we can touch, taste, see, and hear, are just those things in which we are able to discern deeper truths: truths which do not destroy the nature of the thing itself, but allow it to convey something more than just itself.

A language for God

If we live with the reality of God ever about us, that will affect how we see the world. It is a major element of our experience. We cannot be satisfied with explanations about the world which neglect God. Yet, in the seventeenth century, as the world ceased to talk the language of God, and took on the language of science, so explaining the world in religious terms became a more difficult matter. Herbert, again, resorted to homely images to express the otherness of what it was to confront, or be confronted by, God. Glass is a reality. It has a definite composition, and it is possible to keep our eyes fixed on the glass itself, but its nature also allows the one looking to see through it, beyond the mere bunch of particles, however opaque, and by looking beyond, to glimpse more.

A hundred or so years later, poets like Wordsworth and Blake will find words to see God within the very stuff of creation itself, 'to see heaven in a grain of sand', but the seventeenth-century religious writers are still steeped in the mindset of the biblical revelation, which meant that God, while utterly involved in his creation as Creator, and particularly in the life of Jesus Christ, still maintained a significant distance from it. This juggling act of being of creation yet not entirely subsumed in it has, when it comes to the task of description, a significant ally in the use of the image.

The Image

If you have got two major and distinct realities, in our case heaven and earth, and you want to build some sort of bridge between them, the best bridge, for the writer, is the image. You say something is 'like' something else – something that we can handle simply, as if we were a child – and say that the thing that is too abstract to handle, too difficult to see directly, is like this or that. The things of this world give us some clue or hint to another world. For example, we know about light, we can distinguish it from dark. We see light in a candle, or a light bulb, in the sun and moon. Light is an amazing phenomenon and it provides a bridge to our understanding of things beyond our understanding.

Such a use of images is not in the least confined to the seventeenth century. It had been the tool of writers for centuries before that. St John in his Gospel made great use of the image of light, to describe the essence of the nature of the divine, not only because it has the quality of the ungraspable nature of the mystery of God, but also because it is the element which helps us to see the connections. It is both object and facilitator. It is the thing we see, and the thing by which we see, and so corresponds very closely to the nature of God as we fumblingly apprehend him.

If you want to describe something, and writers usually have this urge, then you are involved from the beginning in the business of image-making. A word is an image, a sound picture of a reality greater than itself. The sounds we use for God, 'G', 'o', and 'd', are not God. God is greater and more full of reality than the word we have found it useful to describe him by, but words are one of the best ways we have found to do this difficult job, and we persevere with them. The writers here are in just such a situation. All these writers have set their faith, imaginations, knowledge, and their store of words, at the service of communicating what they have experienced of God. The first response in reading them that comes to my mind is amazement, amazement that they have been in receipt of such experiences, and then a second amazement that they have been able to describe that experience, and then the amazement that that description has been of such immeasurable help to others who have read it.

If 'spiritual writers' seems like an inaccurate phrase for who these people are, then I fear that other definitions may sound, on their own, even more inaccurate. 'Poet' will miss out the area in which their particular genius is at work. 'Divine' is a good seventeenth-century word, but it might confine them to a narrow ecclesiastical sphere. 'Writer', on its own, is too bland and professional, as if writing was merely their bread and butter rather than their gift. Given that the understanding of the phrase 'spiritual writer' is of someone who is trying to bridge the worlds of heaven and earth, and so enter the ordinary and everyday, to lead us into the sphere where the Creator exists, the title 'spiritual writer' might well do.

Christian spirituality

'Behold, I show you a mystery', said St Paul, who is eager not to hide but to reveal. God, in Christ, was eager to reveal himself. Jesus wanted to teach people about the Kingdom of God. There is a whole thrust in the New Testament of things once being in the darkness now brought into the light, with the one caveat that runs through both Old and New Testaments, which is Isaiah's problem of those who do not see and will not understand. With a strong sense of the providence of God at work for those who have eyes to see and hearts to love with, God's will becomes clear, but for others darkness seems inevitable. It is as though in Christ, God was doing all he possibly could to explain the secret, reveal the mystery. Paul, a true servant of Christ, felt a great responsibility to share in this revealing work. We see it as he writes to the church of Colossae: 'I became a servant of the church by virtue of the task assigned to me by God for your benefit: to put God's work into full effect, that secret purpose hidden for long ages and through many generations, but now disclosed to God's people' (Colossians 1.25f).

The interplay in the Gospels between secrecy and revelation is a very interesting one. Jesus asks people not to talk about his miracles. He hides himself from the crowds at times. He speaks in parables, whose message is not immediately apparent to those without faith. His disciples complain to him that he is speaking in riddles, and are relieved when he speaks plainly. Set against all this is the revelation of the mystery that came by his being born and living among the people, dying publicly on the cross, and then revealing himself to the disciples after his death in his resurrected body. There is no simple explanation for this, but the way to understand it better lies in the nature of God as both transcendent and imminent, beyond and among. That paradox, which defies, or passes, all our understanding, is revealed through those images which can contain the truth of both states at once. It is the truth that the early Church struggled with over the nature of the incarnation, both Godhead and manhood, in the one Christ. Truths of this sort are best revealed in a language that helps break the conventional mould of ways of looking at things. It is the miracle of language to reveal the miracle of God's nature. The truths that we cannot capture in prose we can sometimes capture through the combination of rhythm and sense and sound in poetry. Some prose can do that too, and perhaps we should not draw too firm a distinction between prose and poetry, otherwise we get into deep water, but the rhythms of feeling and intuition, when they find a language, speak beyond the ordinary, and can break through into a realm we could call God's Kingdom. So the literary and mystical task is an adventure, a rigorous and challenging one, and our seventeenth-century writers took up that challenge, and by some strange miracle of timing, took up the challenge when language, the English language, seemed to be at its most pliable, creative, and confident of its powers.

Civil War (1642–9)

It would be absurd to write about this period in British civil and spiritual history without making some attempt to see what effect it had on the writers we are looking at here. One of the surprising things about all of them is how little the subject of the war impinges directly on their work. It is almost as if it did not exist: no description of battles, or of the politics behind the war, few, if any, references to the characters at the centre of it. We really could get through the poems and prose of them all without needing to check up a date, or know the plan of a battlefield. It was Rupert Brooke writing about John Donne who said, 'Donne feels only the idea. He does not try to visualize it. He never visualizes, or suggests that he has any pleasure in looking at things. His poems might all have been written by a blind man in a world of blind men' (Hassall, 1956). This is odd, and we might think that they are living in a rarefied, spiritual world which has turned its back on reality.

Dates have a large part to play in this. Lancelot Andrewes (1555–1626) died 15 years before the war, when under James I the religious divisions which partly ignited the conflict were clear, but opposition to the monarchy and the bishops had not yet organized itself. John Donne (1571–1631) died 11 years before the war, and George Herbert (1593–1633) nine years before it. Henry Vaughan (1622–95) and Thomas Traherne (1636–74) lived through it. Vaughan was the most influenced by it, with his brother being killed in the conflict. Traherne was six years old when it started, and 13 when it finished.

Poets do not necessarily feel the need to be journalists, as we understand the term now. Their first aim is not to give a running account of events that are happening in the world around them. What I do think happens with poets and writers is that the tensions in society, and there were different sorts of tensions going on in the first half of the seventeenth century, became obvious not so much through direct references to the divisions that made for war, or to the fighting itself, as was the case with the First World War poets, but they took on the sinuous struggle of the country in their hearts and minds and souls. The poems of Donne, Herbert, and Vaughan are poems of inner conflict and mental turbulence, which echoed the changes and the revolutions that were going on outside their creative selves. They had the passion of a furnace in which tough metals were melting and being reshaped. As the country was beginning to enter a national conflict, so the internal battlefields of these writers were taking on the struggles between science and faith, light and darkness. The prayers of Andrewes are full of a sense of penitence. This must in some way be reflecting his need to shape the national scene in the ways of God, as well as a need for personal transformation. Christopher Hill in his book *Puritanism and Revolution* put it like this:

> The poet has become an isolated individual in a divided society and his mind is divided too. In this broad sense we may speak of a lyric of conflict, whose characteristics are an awareness in the poet's mind of the new and troubling

9

(especially the new scientific discoveries) as well as the old and familiar, and the effort to fit them into a common scheme. (Hill, 1962)

None of these writers lived a charmed life or wrote in an ivory tower. They were writing in times extraordinarily like our own in some ways, dealing with many of the same issues. There was a huge change in ways of communication and the use of language. The translation of the Bible into English was as much a revolution then as information technology is in our own day. The pressure to open up knowledge to the mass of people, in a language which resonates with the everyday world, is an experience common to both centuries. Both are ages of an influential entertainment industry. Between 1580 and 1620 there was a volcanic eruption of plays and the building of theatres, in the same way as television and the cinema have erupted into our own times. The theatres were booming, and Andrewes knew there was stiff competition for audiences. He needed all his powers of rhetoric, and all the passion for communication that Shakespeare, Ben Jonson, and Christopher Marlowe had, and he did not disappoint.

Both are ages of war and violence. In the seventeenth century the Thirty Years War was raging in Europe, and the Civil War in England, Ireland and Scotland was tearing this country apart with scars that we are still able to feel today. Both are centuries in which the advances of science and technology rocked the foundations of traditional beliefs. New discoveries about the universe, a more extensive knowledge of the natural world, mathematics, and medicine, are similar scenarios in both ages. The similarities are strong, and so we have a lot to learn, and a lot to share, but just as important as all of these is the new method of writing poetry that emerged.

The language of the day

It is not surprising that out of the wars of the twentieth century came a new beat, a new rhythm, and a greater intellectual input into poetry. T. S. Eliot, a student of the seventeenth century from his early days at Harvard University, when his lecturer read passages of Donne to the students, found in the

10

rhythms of Donne and Andrewes a voice to speak about the issues that his tumultuous times had brought up. The writers of the early seventeenth century also found a new rhythm, a new intensity, and a greater intellectual involvement in ideas in their poems. They became known as the 'metaphysical' poets. They allied brain to heart, and by a sophisticated use of images that were coming to them from cosmology, astronomy, and science from the writings of people like Francis Bacon, and from the worlds of travel and commerce, with companies being set up in America, 'O my America! my new found land!', they performed alchemical tricks in language which satisfied the hungry mind, and engaged the thirsty soul. We look in vain for the simple sixteenth-century lyrics of the shepherd and his lass. The century of war, and plagues, and self-assertion set the religious mind a more difficult and tortuous task.

A family of writers

These five spiritual writers make a sort of family, and I feel justified in limiting my range to just these for the purpose of this book. Firstly, they are all reasonably well known, and when people have asked me what I have been doing, and I say writing on Donne, Herbert, Andrewes, Vaughan, and Traherne, a look of happy recognition has come over their faces. So, here are a family of writers who please. Secondly, in the family tree, Andrewes seems a foundation spirit, even perhaps a guiding one, in the effect of his spiritual wisdom. His writing we know about, his spiritual counsel we shall never know about fully. He was certainly a great influence on George Herbert, who in turn influenced Henry Vaughan. Donne knew Andrewes and Herbert very well, and the major life changes that both Donne and Herbert went through from court to Church, from the secular to the divine, need researching, and they are periods, certainly in Herbert's life, which are very obscure, but I cannot help feeling that the prayers and holy life of Lancelot Andrewes, possibly mediated through James I, were very significant influences. Vaughan, too, had this retiring, contemplative nature, a love and devotion of the Church of England, and of the primitive Church, which Andrewes promoted by his life and writings. Traherne is, in every sense, later, but he knew Herbert's poetry, and quotes lines from the poem 'Longing' in his recently discovered work 'The Kingdom of God'. Traherne's neo-platonism, and his vocabulary of mystical writing, and the essence in his writings of him being *sui generis*, 'his own man', so to speak, sets him apart from the other four. Yet in his setting at Credenhill, with the church, and the groups of local people, like Susannah Hopton, living devoted and holy lives, I see a connection between Traherne, and the relationship of Herbert to the Ferrars at Little Gidding. This pull between London and the life of the court, and the retiring life of a country parish is very much a part of Herbert's legacy. Given wide parameters, I hope we can usefully say that these five provide a suitable group to hold together, and describe as a family of writers.

Most intensely through the months in the preparation of this book, and more loosely in the years leading up to it, I have collected some images of the seventeenth century which I feed on when inspiration dries up, or my eyes go dizzy in my head. The paintings of the French artist Georges de la Tour adorn my notebook. His strong use of light and shadow, the use of biblical characters, knowing that he was working in the spiritual tradition of Bossuet and Francis de Sales, and the results of this in his beautifully evocative paintings of 'The Penitent Magdalene', are great icons of the controlled passion that made up seventeenth-century devotion.

Then on a summer's afternoon driving through Leicestershire, I stopped off at Staunton Harold, the ancestral home of the Shirleys, and visited the church, built to Caroline principles in the Cromwellian period. This was the retreat of Bp Gilbert Sheldon in the 1650s, to which he brought his copy of Andrewes' prayers, allowing more prayers to be written in for the young Seymour Shirley in order to prepare him for his confirmation. The painted ceiling of the church is full of hidden messages. The woodwork, the heavenly gates, and ironwork still breathe a distinctive air of prayer and ordered worship.

Then there are the box hedges in the inner court of Wilton House, near Salisbury, home of Ann Clifford, whose shelves contained the works of all our writers. I remember, too, the Reverend Ben de la Mare singing his setting of a Herbert poem in Bemerton Church after a day together Herbert

12

hunting, which included a rare visit inside the rectory, and the garden sloping down to the river. The wonderful spiral squiggle at the end of the Dr Williams's Library manuscript of Herbert's poems on the 'F' of *Finis*, and underneath *Soli Deo Gloria*. It was numinous to see the sheer delight of it. On such memories I feed in the lean times, and am very conscious that this account of five great writers is only a very inadequate introduction to people whose works I can hardly wait to get back to, once the ink is dry on this page.

References

Daggy, R. E. (ed.), *Dancing in the Water of Life, The Journals of Thomas Merton*, vol. 5, 1963–1965. Harper, San Francisco, 1997, p. 6.

Hassall, C., *The Prose of Rupert Brooke*. Sidgwick and Jackson, London, 1956, p. 95.

Hill, C., *Puritanism and Revolution*. Mercury Books, London, 1962, p. 341.

Rilke, R. M. (trans. Leishman, J.), *Selected Works*, vol. 2: *Poetry*. The Hogarth Press, London, 1967, p. 312.

1
LANCELOT ANDREWES
1555–1626

If you had been here you would have escaped heats of all sorts, those of the dog-days inclusive. At Downham we never know what heat is. In the city the radiation from so many Walls, against an atmosphere thickened with coal-smoke and fog, makes what is with us a very small puppy (of a dogstar) into a molossiah hound. Come to me, therefore, down here; come if you will, on the day you left us last year, St Augustine's Day.

> Lancelot Andrewes, inviting Isaac Casaubon to stay at
> Downham (Pattison, 1875)

Men believe that their reason governs words.
But it is also true that words, like the arrows
from a Tartar bow, are shot back, and react
on the mind.

> Francis Bacon

It was not until
flesh became word
that he quarried those
audible stones. He
built for his listening God
a cathedral of language.

> Anne Stevenson (1982)

No period of history begins on a completely fresh page. A new chapter depends on all that has gone before. It builds on the past, and certainly makes something new in the process, but old and new live on together. It was so in the seventeenth century. The writers that we are looking at here all contributed something new to the spiritual history of this country, but they were deeply immersed in the spiritual writings of previous centuries. In fact, they made a virtue of gathering together the insights of the past, particularly those of the primitive Church, feeling that they were closer in time and in spirit to the authentic teachings of Jesus. They were also fully conscious of their crucial dependance on the Scriptures, both Old and New Testaments.

No more so than in the writings of Lancelot Andrewes (1555–1626), with whom we begin. Yet, in the English tradition, Andrewes would want to declare his tribute to the thought and writings of that architect of the Church of England, Richard Hooker (1554–1600). Andrewes and Hooker together forged the middle path between the theological extremes of Catholic and Puritan, pointing for their authority to ancient tradition, the power of Scripture, and to moderate notions of common sense. Andrewes was born one year after Hooker, but lived a quarter of a century longer. Andrewes saw James I through his reign, and attended the coronation of Charles I. He was able through this period to maintain the principles that Hooker had established in his great work *Treatise on the Laws of Ecclesiastical Polity*. Indeed, Andrewes saw some of the later books of this work through the hands of the printer, and out into the public domain.

The late sixteenth century was a world in transition. It was moving, at least in this country, from a pre-scientific world, in which Christianity was the dominant religious tradition, to a self-sufficient world, in which God was beginning to be eclipsed by the perceived sense of human achievements in science, commerce, the arts, exploration, and literature. The Renaissance is a title which covers a whole range of social and intellectual changes, and Andrewes has in many ways the feeling of being a Renaissance man. We think we live in a time of change, and in many respects we do, but we often assume we are the only generation ever to have lived in a time of change, forgetting other generations. The breadth of Andrewes' learning was legendary, but it is on two aspects of his genius that I particularly want to concentrate. One is his daily and lifelong concern for prayer, and the other is his world of words. Prayer and words are closely tied together, and transcend the easy definitions of historical moments, and so it is to his spirituality I turn, rather than to his biography, but first, a few pointers to his life would be helpful.

15

Words

Andrewes had the great fortune of good schooling. Richard Mulcaster had recently founded the Merchant Taylors' School in London. Mulcaster had progressive ideas for the time, and was the author of a catechetical work for the young, and a book about his educational theory. Andrewes would have begun his love for languages at school, and of course his commitment to God and to the words about God, in Hebrew, Latin and Greek, the three great biblical languages. A love of language, of words in different languages, and of the meaning and resonances of words, was his early intellectual world. Living near the Thames he must have watched his father, a master mariner, set off for distant countries and longed for his return, partly for the sake of being with his father again, but also because his father would have brought back information and knowledge of yet another language. Andrewes' library contained works in many languages.

In his sermons, Andrewes would often dwell on the world contained within the letters of a word. It was a way of meditating on the truth contained within them. He could take any word in the Bible, in which he would say there are no idle words, and he would spend time thinking about it, seeing its use in other languages, noting, as with a coin, how long it had been in use, and whose image, so to speak, was graven into it, what truth, and what reality it was that lay within it. This was Andrewes' way. It was because he was so much a master of language that when he realized that God had become a little child, and a speechless child at that, he exclaimed, 'The Word that cannot speak a word!'

Hebrew, Latin, and Greek

The very letters themselves had a particular power for him. The Jews in their Scriptures, since pictorial representations of God were forbidden, took to letters to secrete the truths about God. Hebrew, the language of the Old Testament, was a great inspiration for later languages. Greek was the language in which the first records in the New Testament were written down, and was the language of the Eastern Fathers, like St

John Chrysostom, whom Andrewes hugely admired. The well-known, first part of his *Private Prayers* was written in Greek.

Latin needs a book of its own. The first great translation of the Bible into Latin by St Jerome, which was known as the Vulgate, has had an enormous influence on the life of the Church. The Psalms, which Coverdale translated into an English which many still admire, were translated from the Vulgate, and took from the Latin many of their basic words and rhythms. Then there are all the great Latin writers of the early Church, including the extremely influential St Augustine, and many prayers and services which came to the English Church just in Latin, and then into Cranmer's expert and moderate hands, to be turned into English.

In this way language is more than just translated words, it is a living force of communication that God has entrusted to us, and people like Lancelot Andrewes are the craftspeople and the intellects who can communicate afresh to their own generation. Given the treasures of the great biblical languages, and given a period in history when the medieval world was emerging from its dependence on Latin, and finding its own vernacular tongue, in this case English, you would not be surprised to find Lancelot Andrewes at the centre of involvement in the Authorized Version of the Bible.

The Authorized Version

People say that nothing good ever comes from a committee, but the translation of the Authorized Version of the Bible in 1611 came from several committees. The meeting at Westminster Abbey under Andrewes' chairmanship worked on the books from Genesis to 2 Kings. Genesis is thought to have been the work of Andrewes himself.

The Sermons

The excitement of words was all part of that translation work for Andrewes, as of the 96 court sermons that he preached at major festivals to Queen Elizabeth I, and James I. The sermons need a few moments' attention here. If written language was one of Andrewes' great skills, communicating in spoken language was another. He delivered sermons of a quality of language that we would say Shakespeare contributed in his plays. There is no evidence that Andrewes and Shakespeare met, but surely each must have heard of the other in the streets around Southwark, and both had a tremendous store of, and generosity in using, language. They both had so much in their storehouses, and they spent their lives communicating with their treasure: Shakespeare with the whole great tapestry of human life, and Andrewes in the teasing out of the meaning of Scripture. If life was Shakespeare's world, the Bible was Andrewes' world. His sermons show an incredible, encyclopaedic knowledge of the Bible. He must have had almost instant recall of the whole Bible in four languages. We could say he lived in the Bible as others live in large houses, and he knew all the rooms, and connecting passages, its views and its secret places, its occupants, and its neighbours in classical literature.

Prayer

The other major theme in the life of Bishop Andrewes was prayer. We perhaps understand prayer to be something we do for a short time in the morning and evening, or in an emergency when we turn in desperation to God, but for Andrewes, prayer was a life's work. Prayer and life were woven together, and it was even more intimate than that. Prayer was the spirit in which everything was done, 'begun, continued, and ended' in God. The great classic work which gathers the external evidence of his life of prayer is called, by later editors, *Preces Privatae*, or *Private Prayers*. It was not a title that Andrewes used himself, but when his friends realized how much they gained from his method and words in prayer, and translated the notes from Greek, Latin, and Hebrew, and got them printed, they gave the book the title *A Manual of Private Devotions*. When we talk of a book of prayers it conjures up the picture of a book which contains short, organized, petitions to God, crafted and shaped in collect form. If you look for such a system in Andrewes you might be surprised. There is a structure to part of it, but the prayers are only occasionally crafted into small units. A lot of the material might well have been notes for sermons, or private meditations on a text, gathered from different sheets of paper, along with many prayers from the eastern and western traditions of prayer in the Church.

Thomas Merton and Andrewes

Before we open his prayer book, let us jump forward to the twentieth century, and open it with Thomas Merton, the American Trappist monk and writer. In the 1960s Merton moved into a hermitage in the woods, near the monastery, and he used to read the *Private Prayers* of Andrewes during the night. In December 1963, Merton wrote in his diary: 'The reality of death, Donne's poems and Lancelot Andrewes ... it becomes very important to remember that the quality of one's night depends on the thoughts of the day ... I bring there the sins of the day into the light and darkness of truth to be adored without disguise, then I want to fly back to the disguises.' Then he quotes a section from the prayers of Andrewes: 'The heart is deceitful above all things. The heart is deep and full of windings. The old man is covered up in a thousand wrappings.' Merton adds this comment:

> True, sad words: and I would not have felt the truth of them so much if I had not had so much solitude these days, with rain coming down on the roof and hiding the valley. Rain in the night, the murmur of water in the buckets. I cut wood behind the house and enjoy a faint smell of hickory smoke from the chimney while I taste and see that I am deceitful and that most of my troubles are rooted in my own bitterness.
>
> Is this what solitude is for? Then it is good, but I must pray for the strength to bear it. (The heart is deceitful and does not want this, but God is greater than my heart.) (Merton, 1988)

There is a lot in Merton's diaries to help us into the prayers of Lancelot Andrewes. Firstly, we see the need for solitude to absorb them, and the need to take them in small bits and chew over them. Secondly, we notice the way the prayers present themselves without disguise, in much the same way as Scripture has a magisterial openness, a translucence and clarity which is quite shocking to our more devious modern minds. Andrewes' texts have a spirit of glass, in the same way as George Herbert used the term, because we can see through glass 'and there the

19

heavens espy'. Thirdly, we see the way prayer involves us in the
pattern of day and night, the rhythm of light and dark, waking
and sleeping, dying and rising. Thomas Merton found contemplative food in these prayers. Merton the existentialist, whose
greatest horror was the world's destruction of humanity
and humanness, picked out for his diary that amazing line
from Andrewes, 'The old man is covered up in a thousand
wrappings.'

Merton's nights were long in the hermitage, and were a time
of particular poignancy for him. For Andrewes the evening also
gave rise to thoughts of dying and mortality. The first bit of
Andrewes that I copied into my own commonplace prayer
book was this:

> The day has stepped across,
> and for that I thank you, Lord.
> The evening comes,
> give us the gift of light.
>
> As the day has an evening
> so has life.
> Old age is the evening of life,
> age has come to me,
> grant me the gift of joy.
>
> Gone and far off is the day,
> so also is life:
> the life, lifeless.
> The night comes,
> and so does death,
> the death, deathless.
> As the end of the day draws near,
> so too does the end of our life.
>
> Remember us, we pray,
> so that the end of our life
> may be Christian and acceptable,
> faultless, blameless,
> (and if it please you) painless.
> In peace lay us down, Lord, Lord;
> gather us to the feet of your chosen ones,
> when you will, and as you will,

(only apart from shame and sins)
after the checking of the progress of the night
by my doing some good thing.

(Medd, 1892 [Author's translation])

The joints of the day have always been important moments of
prayer for many religions: the dawn and the dusk are particularly resonant of the Christian mystery of dying and rising, so
let us hear one of Andrewes' dawn prayers:

Blessed are you, O Lord our God,
    the God of our forebears
you turn the shadow of death into the morning
and renew the face of the earth:
you roll darkness from the face of the light
and make night to pass, and bring on the day.
You have lightened my eyes that I sleep not in death.
    You have delivered me from the terror by night,
    from the disease that lurks in the darkness.
You have driven sleep from my eyes,
    and slumber from my eyelids;
you make the dawn and dusk to sing for joy
    for I lay down and slept and rose
but you only, Lord, make me dwell in safety.
    I awoke, and look, my sleep was sweet to me.

(Medd, 1892 [Author's translation])

I hesitate to begin to describe the life of Andrewes because it
might then seem that he is not our contemporary. It was T. S.
Eliot, again, who taught the readers of the *Four Quartets* that
history was linked up with the present and the future, 'Time
past and time future are both contained in time present.'
There is something extraordinarily contemporary about
Andrewes, not least in his utter lack of romanticism.

After studying at Pembroke Hall, Cambridge, he became
Vicar of St Giles Cripplegate, a church now surrounded by the
Barbican. He was made a Prebendary of St Paul's Cathedral,
where he lectured, and wandered up and down the aisles,
giving absolution and counsel. He became Dean of Westminster just before George Herbert went to Westminster School as
a boy, but Andrewes and Herbert knew each other well.

21

Herbert arrived and Andrewes, as the newly appointed Bishop of Chichester, was to take up his place in the House of Lords, at Westminster, for the first time, on 5 November 1605. Fortunately the Gunpowder Plot was discovered two days before. From Chichester, Andrewes went to be Bishop of Ely in 1609, and then to be Bishop of Winchester in 1619, until his death in 1626. The Diocese of Winchester then stretched up to Southwark, where he is buried.

The Prayers

What is now gathered into one volume of *Private Prayers* was originally simply a commonplace book, or books. We must not imagine a completed anthology, but a working process, a gathering of texts and prayers from a variety of sources, mainly biblical. There are no manuscripts in Andrewes' own handwriting. There are five manuscripts in existence, but they are thought to be edited copies. More of that later. The volume of prayers would indicate that they are the collection of a lifetime. Andrewes was a very methodical person, and I imagine that he had a system to which he was working, and categories into which he placed whatever new material he found. The editorial work has gone on ever since his day, when his Winchester secretary, Samuel Wright, made a copy, and his former Pembroke Hall colleague, Richard Drake, made an English translation. Books of devotions were a common feature of the time, and Archbishop Laud compiled one. It is assumed that one of the manuscripts in the ownership of Laud was a personal gift to him from Andrewes. This is the famous 'slubbered over' manuscript which is often referred to, and is now in the Bodleian Library, Oxford.

What drew me to the prayers, in the first place, was their structured nature which gives us prayers for each day of the week, starting with the first day (he did not use the pagan names, always referring to first day, second day, and so on). He based the beginning of each day's prayers on the account of the creation in Genesis. We remember that he was responsible for the translation of the Pentateuch, and he lectured extensively on the creation verses in his St Paul lectures, which he delivered in St Paul's, when he was Vicar of St Giles and a prebendary of St Paul's. What an excellent way to begin the day's prayers, by opening up to the created world in all its glory. Let us look at the fourth day (Wednesday):

> Blessed are you Lord,
> who created two sources of light,
> the Sun, the Moon,
> great and less,
> and their stars,
> constellations, the Bear, Orion,
> the Pleiades, the Circle of the Southern Stars,
> and gave them
> light, signs, times,
> Spring, Summer, Autumn, Winter,
> Days, Weeks, Months, Years,
> to rule over day and night.
>
> (Medd, 1892 [Author's translation])

Having opened ourselves out to the created world, we then confess, then pray for, and against, certain things under the headings, intercession, faith, commendation, blessing, and finally, thanksgiving. There is a lot of material for each day, and it was E. B. Pusey in his *Spiritual Letters* who advised a correspondent of 'the need to take them slowly and with lots of pauses' (Pusey, 1901).

At least one-third of the prayers could be described as penitential. The word 'prayers' gives a slightly false impression. We imagine from that word manageable portions of thought directed to God, but what we have are long lists of biblical quotations, placed together, in the creative way that a tapestry is worked. The penitential character of Andrewes' devotions has been a stumbling block to many, and we know from the tenor of *The Book of Common Prayer* that penitence is something that seems to lock us very much into the Reformation period, but the experience of the great saints is that the closer you get to God the more inadequate you feel, regardless of the sins that are an ever present reality in our lives. Perhaps we need to rediscover penitence for ourselves, and see its importance as a way of reflecting not just on our own sin, but also on the sins of the world for which we are, in part, responsible. Pusey again takes up this theme of penitence in his letter of counsel about self-congratulation: 'picture oneself to oneself as something "leprous and defiled, a stinking carcase full of sores from head to foot"' and, 'this Easter-tide we should seek to sink more and more into our own worse than nothingness. "The defiled worm" which Bishop Andrewes calls himself, never rebelled against God's will' (Pusey, 1901). There is one section of the penitential material which reaches depths which Dr Alexander Whyte, the Scottish Presbyterian, described in his edition of the prayers: 'every page pierces us, solemnises us, and subdues us to tears and to prayers and to obedience as no other book of its kind has ever done' (Whyte, 1896).

> No other gift, wealth,
> any of the good things of the world
> can equal tears
> like David's, or Jeremiah's,
> Mary Magdalen's, or Peter's.
> Soft eyes, not hard flint,
> and if I cannot cry on my bed,
> or wash your feet with tears,
> or equal Jeremiah
> or weep with Peter's bitter tears,
> (and O, that I could),
> then can I shake just one felt tear
> into your bottle,
> to be entered into your book.
> If not, then I am pumice, scale, scour.
> How deep must sorry be?
> How much sorry is enough?
> Lend me the tears of Christ,
> from the plenty he shed
> in the days of his flesh.
> O give me some of that store.
> In Christ there are more than enough
> for my less than enough.
>
> (Barrow, 1853 [Author's translation])

(There is a more detailed commentary on this prayer at the end of this chapter, in the examples.)

24

We live in a culture which finds written prayers quite difficult to handle, probably because so many seem antique, and the very contemporary written prayers, in which the soul is bared with embarrassing ease, do not fit easily into the liturgy. But prayers are the closest thing that the Church has to poetry, apart from hymns, and if language is to do anything for us in the Church today it surely must do it through words which help people to pray and relate to God. So how does Andrewes fit into our own world which is so cautious of Tudor devotion? Andrewes wrote his prayers for himself, and so he did not need to worry about their level of communication. He preferred, it seems, to pray in Greek or Latin. Such prayers are obviously difficult for us, because the languages are a barrier, and so the first tool we turn to is that of translation.

Translation

Here I need to describe the work of F. E. Brightman (1856–1932). Brightman was a liturgist and a Canon of Christ Church, Oxford. In his small pamphlet about Brightman, H. N. Bate writes:

> From all Brightman's published work I should single out one small volume as most characteristic of his mind and method – the singularly perfect edition of the Devotions of Bishop Andrewes which was published by Methuen & Company, London, 1903. With Andrewes, Brightman was completely at home and in harmony, in an atmosphere of absorbed devotion, profoundly Catholic, and yet essentially English. Andrewes' mind, like his own, was set upon 'the magnalities of religion', saturated with Scripture, enriched by a wide knowledge of liturgies Eastern and Western, and penetrated by the study of early patristic theology. It was for Brightman a congenial task to trace every clause in the Preces Privatae to its origin, and every allusion to its source. (Procs. British Acad., 1933)

That tells us as much about Andrewes as it does about Brightman. But I sense also a revival of great interest in the prayers of Andrewes in our own day, sparked by Nicholas Lossky's splendid book, not on the prayers but on the sermons of Andrewes.

25

Prayers take on a common ownership after a while, and generally people are not too bothered about who wrote them, as long as they say something they want to say themselves, but have not the words for. I suspect Andrewes himself changed and adapted former prayers, in fact we know he did. Brightman, in his edition of the *Preces Privatae*, notes all the references that he can locate, where Andrewes has used other prayers, and there are a great number of them. The exciting element in all this is the rediscovery of the prayers of Andrewes, and the possibility that gives for producing contemporary translations of prayers that feed from the long tradition of prayers in the English Church. Eric Milner-White, a great anthologizer of prayers himself, wrote in *Liturgy and Worship* (1932) about the *Preces* 'towering above all other books of private devotion, it is the greatest book that Christian and Catholic piety has begotten'. To restore those prayers for our generation will be to effect not only a renaissance of prayer, but also a renaissance of theology rooted in prayer.

The times and the style

Here we need to place Andrewes in his time. He lived, wrote, and thought at a time when the Church of England was taking shape, steering its middle course between the extremes of Roman Catholicism and Genevan Calvinism. He was mining the traditions of the early Church, and the entire Christian history of devotion, East and West, at a time when language, the power of words in the English language, was at its height. This was the age of Shakespeare and the King James Bible. Andrewes himself lived through language. He was a poet-theologian, not in the sense that he wrote poems, but he wrought with language thoughts about God, and entering into the tradition of biblical language he made it so thoroughly his own that he could communicate in no other way. His English prose is legendary, his sermons full of the sinew and thew of the language. David Jones, the Welsh poet and artist, put it like this: 'Been reading Lancelot Andrewes's sermons a bit. Lord, I wish I'd known him before – the tightest English I ever read – so, so good' (Jones, 1980). Whether we will ever be at home enough in language again to enjoy and use Andrewes, I do

26

not know. It has to be said that the style of Andrewes' sermons is quite individual, and the wit, the dexterity of the prose, is not found in the prayers. The prayers are not in English, and rather than being fashioned as gems of poetry in the sense we understand it, they are more reminders, worksheets of thoughts, one word or one thought sets off another in his concordance mind.

The Sheldon Manuscript

I should like to conclude by explaining a little of the work I am doing on Andrewes' prayers at the moment. In 1995, a manuscript of the *Prayers* came into the library at Lambeth Palace. It was known of before, but not by Brightman when he did his edition in 1903. It has a considerable amount of the Latin material that was contained in the first printed edition of Lamphire in 1673. The manuscript came from the ownership of Gilbert Sheldon, Archbishop of Canterbury (1663–77) and is presumed to be his copy of an earlier set of material. It is written in a minute Latin script, very similar to other examples of Sheldon's handwriting. Here is one of the passion prayers from that manuscript, in translation:

> Lord I am wounded in soul,
>   the number,
>   behold the length
>   the breadth
>   the depth of my wounds,
> from the crown of my head
> to the soles of my feet.
>   By your passion, O Lord, heal mine.
>   By your passion, Lord,
> by all the bitterness you suffered,
>   and above all by the love
> which was the cause of your suffering,
> I urge you, ask you, plead with you,
> to offer up all these wounds of mine
> for me, to your Father.

(MS 3708 fol. 12 [Author's translation])

The influence of Andrewes

How is all this going to change the world? It is a question I often ask myself about poetry, as well as about prayer, and the reputation of Andrewes, a man of words and prayer, is under scrutiny here. I am not sure prayer or poetry has to be judged first on its ability to change anything. It is more to be seen as an indication of the way a person is changing under the influence of the Holy Spirit in their inner life, hid with God. Prayers are the fascinating outworking of a soul in motion. We see through prayer into the very heart of the believer. We see their priorities, their longings, their fears and joys. Prayers mark out the passion of faith. Prayer, said Thomas Aquinas, is the language of desire.

In the debate about Andrewes' stature as a saint, there is some doubt as to whether his life was benevolent enough. In one or two cases recorded, he seemed less than kind, more political and distant than might be expected of a saint. In many respects, his life, like most of ours, was not an exact imitation of the life of Christ, but Nicholas Lossky has other grounds for his sanctity:

There are those who, in the secret of the heart, grow by prayer, nourished and watered by the Word and Sacrament of the Church. They enter more and more deeply into the deified humanity of Christ, by the Spirit who dwells in their heart. Christ has assumed the whole of humanity. He is the complete man who recapitulates humanity. Men and women who consecrate their lives to prayer grow little by little to a Christic dimension of a humanity responsible for the whole of creation. And the more they grow, the more they recognize themselves as sinners before God.

The Preces Privatae, by this permanent intercession for all that Lancelot Andrewes knew of the world of his time (and of all time, for his prayer has a Eucharistic dimension) gives an indication that his interior biography is an example of this type of experience.

In our humble opinion, it is right that the new sanctorale of the liturgical calendar of the Church of England has allotted the 25th September to Lancelot Andrewes, Bishop of Winchester, 1626. (Lossky, 1991)

Examples

Sermon on the Resurrection, 1620 (John 20.16)
'All green on the sudden'

Ninety-six of Andrewes' sermons were published shortly after his death at the request of Charles I. One of the final injunctions of Charles to his family was to read the sermons of Lancelot Andrewes. Since that time, people's estimate of them has been various. Owen Chadwick's article in *Theology*, 'A Defence of Lancelot Andrewes' Sermons' (November/December 1999) has contested the value of some of the criticism that was levelled at them during the seventeenth century by Aubrey, Fuller, and Birch. *Seventeen Sermons on the Nativity* was published at the end of the nineteenth century in the Ancient and Modern Library of Theological Literature, and it was this edition that sparked T. S. Eliot's interest in the sermons, and led him to quote parts of them in his poems, particularly in 'Journey of the Magi', 'Ash-Wednesday' (1930), and 'Gerontion'.

In the book referred to above, there is an extensive and masterly overview of the sermons. It is fascinating to see how an Orthodox scholar like Lossky sees into the mind of Andrewes, who was himself so much influenced by the theology and liturgy of the Orthodox Church, through the writings of the Eastern Fathers.

As Owen Chadwick has described, there have been criticisms of the sermons: 'He did play with his text, as a jackanapes does, who takes up a thing and tosses and plays with it, and then takes up another and plays a little with it. Here's a pretty thing and there's a pretty thing' (John Aubrey); 'his artificial amble' (Thomas Fuller); 'that vicious taste' (Thomas Birch).' In our own time, an age of sound-bites and visual images, the sermons have been found to be too wordy, intellectual, and convoluted. Others, who have given them time, have found great inspiration in them. Arthur Pollard put it like this:

> Andrewes is a kind of ecclesiastical linguistic analyst, an exegete, not content until he has squeezed the last drop of meaning out of a word. He is concerned with the derivation

of words rather than with their poetry. Donne combined weight with grace, learning with emotional power. Andrewes, less versatile, appealed more exclusively to the intellect. (Pollard, 1963)

Putting aside the problem of finding them in the first place, because of the sermons' intense scholarship and tightly packed thought they are not easily approached. The sermons have to be taken slowly and each sentence, indeed each word, needs thought, to yield up its value. A structure to each sermon there certainly is, and indeed had to be, to help along the concentration and memories of the congregations who listened to them. There is passion too, although, as Pollard said, their emotional range is not as great as Donne's.

Let us take, as an example to look at more closely, and as the basis for discussion, the last part of Andrewes' Easter sermon of 1620, preached in the presence of King James I, who was a great admirer of Andrewes' sermons, at Whitehall on Easter Sunday, 16 April 1620. The sermon was based on the text from St John's Gospel, chapter 20, verses 11 to 16. It was about the visit of Mary Magdalen to the empty tomb, her worried search for the body of Jesus, and her discovery of the risen Lord in the garden. As a setting for the delivery of the sermon we have to imagine Andrewes preaching from a pulpit surrounded by a lot of people, for his sermons gathered the crowds, and above him, and looking down from the balcony, was the King and his entourage. After the sermon, at the conclusion of Morning Prayer, the King would descend, and parting the congregation as if it was the Red Sea, would go forward to receive his Easter Communion, and then return to the balcony upstairs. It must have been a very grand and dramatic occasion.

This is a sermon which lends itself to dramatization. Andrewes has entered into the feelings of the characters, particularly into Mary Magdalen's feelings, more than in any other sermon I know. Because of this, I thought it would be helpful to divide the text up, without losing any of it except the Latin, which Andrewes usually translates as he goes along anyway, and to assign it to particular voices or characters. The voice of Andrewes holds centre stage, and Mary Magdalen is allowed to react with Andrewes. I have invented two characters from the presence of the two angels at the tomb, and turned them into gardeners. In the sermon the theme of the garden as an image of resurrection is very strong, and so gardeners seemed appropriate voices. They also allow Andrewes' irony, and even humour, to come alive. I hope Andrewes, or purists in our day, will not mind me reshaping the sermon in this way, and that you, the reader, will benefit from some variation in how you hear a sermon. It will also give small groups the opportunity to have an active participation in the sound and the thought of the text.

Reader	'Jesus saith to her "Mary": She turned herself, and said to him Rabboni; that is to say, Master.'
Andrewes	Nothing so allures, so draws love to it, as doth love itself. In Christ specially, and in such, in whom the same mind is. For, when her Lord saw, there was no taking away His 'taking away' from her, all was in vain, neither men, nor angels, nor himself . . .
Gardener 1	So long as he kept himself Gardener –
Andrewes	Could get anything of her, but . . .
Magdalen	My Lord is gone, he is taken away . . .
Andrewes	And that for the want of Jesus, nothing but Jesus could yield her any comfort: He is no longer able to contain, but even discloses himself by his voice, in the wonted accent of it, does but name her name.
Jesus	Mary.
Andrewes	No more and that was enough. That was as much as to say she would at least take notice of him. That shewed he was no stranger, by calling her by her name. For whom we call by their names, we take particular notice of. So Christ, Mary Magdalen. And indeed this is the right way to know Christ, to be known of him first.
Gardener 2	For till he knows us, we shall never know him aright.
Andrewes	And now, lo, Christ is found . . .

31

Gardener 1	Found alive that was sought dead.
Gardener 2	A cloud may be so thick we shall not see the sun through it. The sun must scatter that cloud, and then we may. Here is an example of it. It is strange, a thick cloud of heaviness had so covered her, as, see Him she could not through it.
Gardener 1	This one word, these two syllables.
Jesus	Mary.
Gardener 2	From his mouth, scatters it all.
Gardener 1	No sooner had his voice sounded in her ears, but it drives away all the mist, dries up her tears, lightens her eyes.
Magdalen	Then I knew him straight . . . Rabboni.
Gardener 2	If it had lien in her power to have raised him from the dead she would not have failed, but done it, I dare say.
Gardener 1	Now it is done to her hands.
Magdalen	And with this all is turned out and in. A new world now.
Andrewes	Away with 'they have taken him away'. His taking away is taken away quite. For if his taking away were her sorrow: if sad for his death, for his taking away –
Magdalen	Then glad for his rising, for his restoring again.
Andrewes	Surely, if she would have been glad but to have found but his dead body –
Magdalen	And she finds it, and Him alive –
Andrewes	What was her joy? He that was thought lost . . .
Magdalen	Is found again.
Andrewes	And found not as he was sought for, not a dead body –
Magdalen	But a living soul, nay, a quickening spirit then.
Andrewes	And that might you well say.
Magdalen	He shewed it, for he quickened me and my spirits, that were as good as dead.
Andrewes	You thought you should have come to Christ's resurrection today . . .

Magdalen	And so you do. But not to his alone, but even to my resurrection too. For in very deed, a kind of resurrection it is, is wrought in me; revived as it were and raised from a dead and drooping, to a lively and cheerful estate. The Gardener has done his part, made me all green on the sudden.
Andrewes	And all this by the word of his mouth. Such power is there in every word of his; so easily are they called, who Christ will but speak to . . . (*The bells begin again*)
Andrewes	And in his good time (as shall be expedient for us) vouchsafe every one of us, as he did Mary Magdalen in the text, to know him and the virtue of his resurrection; and make us partakers of both, by both hearing and seeing, by his blessed Word, by his holy mysteries, the means to raise our souls here, the pledges of the raising up of our bodies hereafter. Of both which he makes us partakers, who is the author of both, Jesus Christ, the righteous.

The Story of Magdalen in the Garden

Andrewes powerfully uses the story of Mary Magdalen as an archetype of a journey through faith, despair, and back to faith again. Magdalen was drawn to Christ in her life because she had experienced the loving power of forgiveness through him. This made her devoted to him, but firstly the crucifixion took him away from her as a living being, and secondly his corpse was taken away from the tomb. She was desperate to find what she had lost. She was in turmoil and despair, but she continued to search. She did not give up, and her search was rewarded. Jesus came to her. His 'taking away from her' was itself, quite 'taken away'. There is much play on this 'taking away', the phrase is repeated over and over again, as Magdalen herself repeated it many times. We must remember it was the age of puns, words which allow for a double meaning, in different contexts. Jesus was taken away, then he was brought back, and so his taking away was taken away. We no doubt experience times of faith and times of despair. The story of Mary Magdalen, at such times, is one for us.

The saying of the name

The saying of Mary's name by Jesus came with a tremendous power. He spoke it in his 'wonted', or familiar, accent. Jesus takes the initiative, although Mary had been calling hard herself. 'The right way to know Christ is to be known of him first.' Yet there is a lead-up. Our first knowledge is our experience of the call, but it could be that in all sorts of ways, this call has been prepared for by the love and prayers of others, of family, of church, and the call is the moment when all things momentarily coalesce, come together. We then become personally involved, because our name is named. St Paul's experience and his thinking were largely formed by this pattern. The call of God and our acceptance come together: grace and faith meet halfway.

The Darkness

Magdalen was in the dark over the whereabouts of her beloved Jesus. This experience of darkness is very common, of failing to experience God's presence, of being in a 'cloud of unknowing'. It can last for a lifetime. 'The sun must scatter that cloud and then we may' see God, but perhaps that will only happen after this life. The Word scatters the darkness, and the Word is both Christ, as in St John's prologue, and on a very simple level, the voice of Jesus saying 'Mary', 'this one, these two syllables. Mary. From his mouth, scatters it all. No sooner had his voice sounded in her ears, but it drives away all the mist, dries up her tears, lightens her eyes. Then she knew him straight ... Rabboni.'

Private Prayers

Give me tears

Should God forgive?
   No.
I am sorry
   but not enough.
Would that I were more,   5
would be glad if I were more,
sorry that I am not more,

for I wish that I could more,
and I grieve that I can no more.
   Yes,   10
my lack of grief needs grieving for.
   Who will help me be sorry?
   Myself,
   but it's not in me
     not in my power.   15
I know I should be more sorry,
   and I know that I have the will to be sorry,
   but I cannot do it.

Lord, give. It is in you to give,
    like rock into water,   20
   give me tears, make a fountain of my head,
    give me the grace of tears.
   Drop down you heavens from above and rain
    on the dryness of my desert.

   Give, Lord, this grace.   25
No other gift,
not great riches
nor any of the good things of the world,
can equal the grace of tears,
   like David's, or Jeremiah's,   30
   or Mary Magdalen's, or Peter's
    (his, in bitterness).

Make my eyes to weep,
   leave them not like hard flint . . .

but, if you will, one drop at least,   35
and then another as well,
for your bottle,
for the book.

But what if I can't manage even that?
Oh, pumice!   40
Oh! lime, boiling
in freezing water . . .
At least of Christ's tears,
grant me some.

(Lambeth Palace Ms. 3708 fols 31, 32 [Author's translation])

NOTES

Line 17 Romans 7.18, 'For I know that nothing good dwells in me –
my unspiritual self, I mean – for though the will to do good is
there, the ability to effect it is not.'

Line 20 Psalm 114.8, '[The God of Jacob] turned the rock into a pool
of water, the flinty cliff into a welling spring.' Look also at Exodus
17.6.

Line 21 Jeremiah 9.1, 'Would that my head were a spring of water,
my eyes a fountain of tears.'

Lines 21–22 Here we can see a close relationship between the prayer
and the section on tears in Andrewes' *Sermons on Repentance, 1619*:
'This too we can wish with the prophet and so let us wish "O that
my head were full of water and my eyes fountains of tears", to do it
as it should be done! This we can. And pray we can, that He which
"turneth the flint stone into a springing well" would vouchsafe us,
even as dry as flints, the grace of tears, as the Fathers call it, some
small portion of that grace to that end. Though weep we cannot,
yet wish for it and pray for it we can.'

Line 23 Isaiah 45.8.

Lines 30, 31 Again from *Sermons on Repentance, 1619*: 'David's eyes
gushed out with water, he all to wet his pillow with them: Mary
Magdalen wept enough to have made a bath. We urge not these.
But if not pour out, not gush forth, shall not our eye afford a drop
or twain?'

There is here such a close connection between prayer and
sermon, it fascinates me to wonder which came first. Were his
sermon notes done as prayers? Or did he simultaneously think
and write publicly and privately? The sermon is more measured,
more didactic, more aware of an audience or a congregation.

There is a telling phrase in this part of the sermon on weeping, just four words which open the door a chink into the place of prayer, which would not be part of the prayer, and they are these: 'Who can weep when he lists? I know it well, they be the overflowings of sorrow'; Andrewes in his sermon indicates that he has experienced the grace of tears but they have come without being forced.

Line 41 The strange image of lime, for emotion, has to do with the contrary nature of lime in and out of water: 'Out of water, where they should be hot, no heat appears in them; in water, where they should be cold, there they boil and take on' (Sermon for Ash Wednesday, 1624). Basically, lime does not do what you expect it to, and the same is true of tears. They don't always, if ever, come when you want them to, because they are the result of the emotions, not of the reason. Herbert also uses the image, in his poem, 'The Glimpse':

> Lime begged of old (they say)
> A neighbour spring to cool his inward heat;
> Which by the spring's access grew much more great.

What was engineered to cool, in fact, by the glimpse, grows more fierce.

Line 43 To see another example of how Andrewes' prayers and sermons feed each other, take the last line about Christ helping, by providing his own tears. 'At least of Christ's tears grant me some', which in *Sermons on Repentance, 1619* is expressed like this: 'And lastly, this we can, even humbly beseech our merciful God and Father, in default of ours, to accept of the strong crying and bitter tears which in the days of his flesh his blessed Son in great agony shed for us (Hebrews 5.7); for us, I say, that should, but are not able to do the like for ourselves, that what is wanting in ours may be supplied from thence.'

We are familiar with Shakespeare's soliloquies, which are private thoughts spoken aloud. Here in Andrewes' prayers, we find ourselves very much in the soliloquy tradition. It is difficult to say how much Andrewes wanted his prayers to be made public, or published. We believe he gave some organized prayer schemes to friends, as in the famous gift of a copy of the Greek prayers to Bishop Laud, shortly before Andrewes died. Other prayers may have been found after his death among his papers, and gathered together for publication by his secretary and friends. Andrewes had a wide reputation for learning and sanctity, and his literary remains would have been of interest to many. As I have tried to suggest earlier, the history of the manuscripts is complex and rather hidden in obscurity.

This passage from the Sheldon manuscript, selected for commentary, comes to us only in Latin in manuscript form, but it has been known from printed versions and been translated into English. This particular translation is mine and not entirely literal, but I have tried to give it a bit more urgency and immediacy than some other translations have.

What do we make of it? It is about feeling sorry for our sins, or penitence, and it comes as part of a much longer penitential section in the *Private Prayers*. It is, perhaps, surprisingly long to us, perhaps even unnaturally long. Why go on battering at heaven's gate like this?

There are at least four possible lines of enquiry. One is that Andrewes really did have something to be extremely sorry about, an event, an accident, a sin which haunted him. Alexander Whyte suggests it may have been as a result of Andrewes' part in the Essex affair, a complex matrimonial dispute, a divorce case, in which King James asked Andrewes to go against his better judgement, because the reputation of King James' favourite, the Earl of Essex, was at stake. Whyte makes much of this affair:

> Sometimes one single sin will still leave its mark on a man long long after it has been forsaken, repented of, atoned for, and forgiven . . . The Essex case followed Andrewes about all his days, as his drunkenness followed Noah, and his adultery David, and the sins of his blasphemy and injuriousness Paul, and our sins us. (Whyte, 1896)

That is one possibility.

Another thought is that Andrewes had an extremely scrupulous conscience, and he needed to be really honest with himself. In addition to these two possibilities, we must remember that Andrewes had the whole of the biblical material on penitence at his fingertips, and one quotation, one biblical character, immediately suggested another, and so the lament grew. It is a form of prayer that Anselm, Abbot of Bec and later Archbishop of Canterbury, used in his long meditative prayers written to the saints, such as to St Peter, to the Blessed Virgin Mary, and

St Mary Magdalen. The prayer addressed to St Mary Magdalen begins:

> St Mary Magdalene
> you came with springing tears,
> to the spring of mercy, Christ;
> from him your burning thirst was abundantly
> refreshed;
> through him your sins were forgiven;
> by him your bitter sorrow was consoled.
>
> (Ward, 1973)

Another possibility is that the prayers and the sermons were in some way brought about together. There is a strong textual relationship between them, as we shall see from the notes, but we shall have to do some intricate detective work to discover whether the sermons were the springboard for the prayers, or the other way round, and of course, whether behind both there was not only a teaching motive, but a personal motive, by which it had to be like that, to be true to Andrewes' real experience.

It may help you to consider how you react to tears, and in what way you cry out to God, if at all, and what images of grief and despair you naturally turn to. Here, with Andrewes, it is dryness and irrationality, an inability to shed tears when they might be most expected, but there are many other words and pictures, such as darkness, loneliness, rejection, and bleak weather. The poet Gerard Manley Hopkins uses a similar image to Andrewes when he cries out, 'O thou lord of life, send my roots rain.' You may also like to think about the difference between guilt and penitence, and how guilt seems to shut doors, whereas penitence, in the presence of a loving and forgiving God, redeems, and opens up possibilities for a fresh start, and a new life.

Writing Prayers

'A cold coming we had of it'

With the increasing number of lay people, as well as clergy, now involved in leading the intercessions, there is the need to think carefully about what it is we are doing, and to have help in the process of constructing prayers. The public aspect of this makes it doubly important, because those leading the prayers are having to communicate to a wide range of people in a Sunday morning congregation. We do not want to make it so special that no one feels worthy to do it, or comes forward to help, or even worse if we do not value the contribution of those who plead falteringly, but from the heart. All I say is that it is worth seeing how a mind, steeped in prayer, comes at the job. So, how did Lancelot Andrewes construct his prayers?

First of all, his prayers came out of his faith. It was natural for him to place his thinking about matters of daily life at the disposal of God, and it was his habit to write those prayers down. That makes us pause for a while and ask, why did Lancelot Andrewes need to write so much down? First he was a bishop, and no doubt had occasion to lead people in public prayer, not only from *The Book of Common Prayer*, but also in moments when the King asked him to pray on, or for, a particular occasion. For example, 'A Form of Prayer with Thanksgiving, to be used yearly upon the fifth day of November, for the happy deliverance etc. . . .' was a prayer which Andrewes was asked to write, the purpose of which was obvious:

> Accept also, most gracious God, of our unfeigned thanks for filling our hearts again with joy and gladness, after the time that thou hadst afflicted us, and putting a new song into our mouths . . .

But apart from the public occasions there were the prayers he needed for less formal times, when his heart and his pen turned to a few words needed for those going on a journey.

Before we look at Andrewes' prayer on this subject, let us spend a moment thinking how we ourselves would phrase a prayer at the beginning of a journey. A group of pilgrims are setting off to Iona, Lindisfarne, Rome, or Compostella. Or, again, a family is setting off for a new life in a country far away, and they have asked us to say a prayer. We would want to begin, no doubt, with an address to God, and then simply ask God for whatever we want, a good journey, a safe journey.

As we begin to think in the presence of God, we begin to think what it is that we really want from God, 'his presence

ever about us, at the beginning, in the middle, and at the end',
'that we may make best use of the journey, it's not just the arriving'. We will want to pray for those people we might meet on
the way, the people we leave behind, those people who will
help us, drive us, fly us, or pilot us. There are many things that
pour into our minds that we want to express in the presence of
God.

How did Andrewes' mind work with prayers? Take his
'Prayer for a Journey'. The most important thing that
Andrewes did after placing himself at the disposal of God, was
to engage his concordance mind, much as we would sit at a
computer, and type in the word 'journey'. When Andrewes
thought of a journey, he went first to the great journeys of the
early books of the Old Testament. His opening words in the
prayer are the words of Abraham's servant who travelled to
Aram-maharaim, where Nahor lived. The servant prayed,
'Lord God of my master Abraham, give me good fortune this
day.' Quite simple really. After that opening address, Andrewes
turns to the prayer of Moses in Exodus 35.15: 'Moses said to the
Lord, "Indeed if you do not go yourself, do not send us up from
here."' That is, if you are not coming, I am not going! Put those
two short prayers together, and we have the beginnings of a
prayer:

> O Lord God of my father Abraham, and of Moses,
>   give me good fortune this day,
> and indeed, if you are yourself not with me,
>   do not send me out from here.

You see how powerful the ideas, and the prayer itself, become,
when the voices and experience of the great travellers for God
speak for us. Andrewes felt that, and knew it in his bones. His
prayer came from his faith in God, and in the revelation of
God's purposes in Scripture.

Now see the rest of his short prayer and notice Andrewes'
deep dependence on the biblical tradition, both for his general
ideas and for his words. It is interesting again to note the words
which are not biblical, and hear the rhythms and the ideas
Andrewes himself used when, in a sense, working on his own
material. His mind often works in threes, even in the smallest
phrases, as it is here:

bring me on my way,
bring me to my journey's end,
bring me home again.

Here is all of it, in the Brightman translation of 1903:

A Prayer before a Journey

Send me good speed this day:
if thy presence go not with me,
   carry me not up hence.
Thou who didst speed the way
   of Abraham's servant ⎫   ⎧ an angel
   of the Wise Men   ⎭ by the leading of ⎩ a star

Thou who didst preserve
   Peter amid the waves,
   Paul in shipwreck:
be with me, O Lord, and speed my way:
bring me on my way,
bring me to my journey's end,
bring me home again.

(Brightman, 1903)

The Journey of the Magi

One of the most famous passages in Andrewes' Sermons comes from his 1622 Christmas Day sermon. It has become famous through its use by T. S. Eliot at the beginning of his poem 'Journey of the Magi'. In the light of our thinking about journeys, the most important journey becomes the journey towards Christ. The point of all journeys, and their end, lies in the will of God. The Feast of the Epiphany celebrates the end of the journey for the Gentile Kings, when they saw the Christ child, having undergone so much on the journey.

A part of Andrewes' 1622 Christmas Day sermon

A cold coming they had of it at this time of the year, just the worst time of the year to take a journey, and specially a long

42

journey in. The ways deep, the weather sharp, the days short, the sun farthest off, the very dead of winter . . .

And these difficulties they overcame, of a wearisome, irksome, troublesome, dangerous, unseasonable journey; and for all this they came. And came it cheerfully and quickly, as appeareth by the speed they made. It was but 'we saw, we came', with them; they saw, and they came, no sooner saw, but they set out presently. So as upon the first appearing of the star, as it might be last night, they knew it was Balaam's star; it called them away, they made ready straight to begin their journey this morning. A sign they were highly conceited of His birth, believed some great matter of it, that they took all these pains, made all this haste that they might be there to worship Him with all the possible speed they could. Sorry for nothing so much as that they could not be there soon enough, with the very first, to do it even this day, the day of His birth. All considered, there is more in 'they came', than shews at the first sight. It was not for nothing it was said in the first verse, 'behold, they came'; their coming hath a behold on it, it well deserves it. And we, what should we have done? Sure these men of the East shall rise in judgement against the men of the West (Matt. 8.11), that is us, and their faith against ours in this point. With them it was but 'we saw, we came'; with us it would have been but 'we shall come', at most. Our fashion is to see and see again before we stir a foot, specially if it be to the worship of Christ. Come such a journey at such a time? No; but fairly have put it off to the spring of the year, till the days longer, and the ways fairer, and the weather warmer, till better travelling to Christ.

Interlude

A Letter

to Bp Lancelot Andrewes from Mr George Herbert
1618/1619

To Lanc. Andrewes, Bishop

Most holy father,

I came back from Cambridge, straight from the comfort of
your presence, feeling myself a few inches bigger, and spiri-
tually the more fulfilled from sheer joy. For, what reason had I
to stay? Your approval gave me the wherewithal for the
journey: that approval could in fact have supported a much
longer expedition.

I am now overwhelmed with university work, so it has not
been easy to carve this slice of time from these duties. That is
not to say that my heart is not full of you to the extent of yearn-
ing to devote myself to every little service which my little self
can offer; it is rather that I beg you to forgive the way my pen
is taken up with other matters – a pen, which, even if it was
given a holiday from all those duties, could not hammer out
anything approaching your standard of perfection. Be that as
it may, you are so gentle and understanding that you will not
misinterpret my delay in writing these lines to you, nor think
that, after starting with all the enthusiasm of a youthful infatuation, rather than being attracted by a carefully considered,
mature judgement, my love for you has now lost all the great
warmth it had, and is now buried in its silence; the picture I
have in my mind is one of those rather feeble breaths of air
which wake up at the first hint of warmth and then, when they
have risen a little, grow cold and eventually sink back to where
they began. This indeed is apt to happen to those who run with
eager haste after their affections, keeping pace with them, and
then let themselves be blown hither and thither with every
change of wind.

I did not creep into your approval without careful thought. I
judged your love for me and mine for you quite properly; I
articulated them and weighed them carefully. When I had

applied all the force of my thinking to my life and had shar-
pened the view of myself by looking at myself in the light of
your qualities, I came to a point in my reflections, after travelling from you to me and me to you, where I decided that I must
never stop, never tire, until I had either found or created some
'Milky Way' to the shining brilliance of your mind. My enthusiasm was never blunted by the thought that I was really a
nobody; for this was how I saw it: if I were so mean an object
that, even with all my utmost efforts and unflagging attention,
I could not rise above the unfavourable cold assessment from
others, and chip off for myself even some fragments from the
vast block, in all its greatness, of your integrity and intellectual
accomplishments, which are for all to see in you – if all the
promise of real achievement arising from my attentiveness to
you and from my studies sinks back to this, then 'why struggle
to be somebody of poor reputation when I could win favour
from the public by silence?' But that is not, it seems, how it is;
for all my hopes are being realized, the door is open and I have
been welcomed into the circle of your favour; and I shall always
most gratefully recognize that this has happened more by
virtue of your gracious and sensitive kindness than through
any deserts of mine. Indeed, my prayer will be that I be banished from any share in the light of day, inasmuch as it is
shared with you, should I even stop acknowledging what I
owe to your undeserved kindness.

In spite of all that, I beg you, Father, to allow me to indulge
the expectations of men, ever so little, and walk just that much
less in the broad acres of Winchester, while I perform two
heavy responsibilities among my folk here – that is to say,
being Praelector of Rhetoric this year, and Orator for this and
the subsequent years – at least while I do my duty by rhetoric.
Although I would not want to be given even 600 little holdings
of this sort in exchange for your gracious favour, yet I think it a
greater shame to fall short in a public than in a private service,
and that the sin of dishonouring an obligation has wider implications than that of neglecting one. In Cambridge I am tied by
obligation; with you I am bound also, but with gentler bonds
and ones which love often loosens. In Cambridge my task is
more one of necessity, in Winchester infinitely more one of pleasure and loftiness of theme. What the philosopher wrote about

45

touch and vision, could quite properly be applied to my
situation.

The time is approaching when I can throw off one of the two
yokes and thus, with half my burden taken off me, I shall return
to paying my respects to your exalted position. I shall do so
feeling freer and more easily able to straighten my back than
now; I shall gain inspiration from the very release from duty.
Meanwhile, I want you to appreciate that there is nothing in
the possession of the human race which burns with a stronger
love than does my breast; nor does any understanding, in so
far as it touches not the heart but the head, diminish, let alone
dissolve, your rights as lord over me. Along with my university
appointments which are maternal I have taken upon myself the
service of my Father. 'As much as those things grow so much
you, my love, will grow.' If you believe that sentence and, with
your accustomed generosity, respect truth in all its guises, you
will make me happy 'with an extra measure of blessing', truly
happy.

Your devoted and loyal son, George Herbert.

PS Please forgive me, distinguished hero, that my terms of
address walk so boldly in this letter. I could have filled line
upon line with your titles and obsequious forms of address,
but, in my view, Roman style and its traditional 'periodic'
rhythm forbids that. It is for that reason that I preferred to
defer to the way that you like to hear prose – concise and well
polished – than to indulge the extravagance of the age and the
swelling cancer of currying favour which has not been sufficiently cured by our excellent King from growing ever more
turgid and pretentious by the day.

(The date of this letter can be approximately determined by the
reference to Herbert being engaged both in Rhetoric and in
Orator's business, though expecting shortly to be free from the
former. He was appointed Praelector in Rhetoric on 11 June
1618, the duties probably to begin from the Michaelmas term
and to continue for one year. He was appointed deputy Orator
on 21 October 1619, and already in September he was preparing a Latin oration: the rhetoric lectures were prescribed to be

in English. Andrewes was translated from Ely to Winchester in Feb 1618/19.)

The letter of George Herbert to Lancelot Andrewes, which in the text here has been translated into English, in its original Latin form is found in Hutchinson. Translation from the Latin into English was kindly made for me by the Revd Christopher Turner. The English translation has not been published before in this form.

Editions

PRAYERS

The prayers of Lancelot Andrewes are best read in the edition by Brightman, F. E., *The Private Devotions of Lancelot Andrewes*, Methuen, 1903. This is now out of print but secondhand copies are usually obtainable. A shorter edition of this work was published as Brightman, F. E., *The Preces Privatae of Lancelot Andrewes*, edited with an introduction by A. E. Burn, Methuen, 1908. This is the edition that first fell into my hands.

SERMONS

The 96 sermons are available only in rather ancient editions, but the five volumes of sermons, in the 11-volume edition of Andrewes' Works, in the Library of Anglo-Catholic Theology, ed. J. P. Wilson and James Bliss, Oxford, 1841–54, are usually obtainable from theological libraries.

Seventeen Sermons on the Nativity, published by Griffith, Farran, Browne & Co., Ltd, undated, but probably in the 1890s, is available secondhand. This was the edition that T. S. Eliot worked from.

More recently *Lancelot Andrewes, Selected Writings*, selected by P. E. Hewison, Carcanet, 1995, is in print. This includes selections of sermons, including the full text of the Christmas Day sermon 1622. There is also a short selection of the prayers.

References

Bacon, F., *The Essays or Counsels Civil and Moral*. Oxford World Classics, Oxford University Press, Oxford, 1999.

Bacon, F., *Essays or Counsels Civil and Moral*, Simpkin, Marshall, Hamilton, Kent & Co. Ltd, London, undated.

Barrow, J. (ed.), *Preces Privatae Quotidianae, Lanceloti Andrewes*. Library of Anglo-Catholic Theology, John Henry Parker, Oxford, 1853, p. 378 (author's translation).

Bate, H. N., 'Frank Edward Brightman (1856–1932)', *Proceedings of the British Academy*, 19 (1933), pp. 345–50.

Brightman, F., *The Private Devotions of Lancelot Andrewes*. Methuen, London, 1903, pp. 260, 261.

Chadwick, O., 'A Defence of Lancelot Andrewes' Sermons', *Theology*, November/December, 1999, pp. 431–35.

Hutchinson, F. E. (ed.), *The Works of George Herbert*. Oxford University Press, Oxford, 1941, pp. 471–73.

Jones, D., *Dai Greatcoat*. Faber, London, 1980, p. 88.

Lossky, N., *Lancelot Andrewes the Preacher (1555–1626)*. Clarendon Press, Oxford, 1991, pp. 26–27.

Medd, P. G., *The Greek Devotions of Lancelot Andrewes*. London, 1892, p. 167 (author's translation).

Medd, p. 14 (author's translation).

Medd, p. 77 (author's translation).

Merton, T., *Vow of Conversation*. Ed. Burton Stone, N., The Lamp Press, Basingstoke, Hants, 1988, pp. 107, 109.

Milner-White, E., 'Modern Prayers and their Writers'. In Lowther Clarke, W. K. (ed.), *Liturgy and Worship*, SPCK, London, 1932, p. 751.

MS 3708 fol. 12 in the Lambeth Palace Library (author's translation).

Pattison, M., *Isaac Casaubon 1559–1614*. Longmans, Green and Co., London, 1875, p. 396.

Pollard, A., *English Sermons*, Writers and their Work: no. 158. Longmans, Green and Co. (for the British Council), London, 1963, pp. 13–14.

Pusey, E. B., *Spiritual Letters of Edward Bouverie Pusey*. Ed. Johnson and Newbolt, Longmans, Green and Co., London, 1901, pp. xiv, 43, 109.

Stevenson, A., *Minute by Glass Minute*. Oxford University Press, Oxford, 1982, p. 35 (from the poem 'Lancelot Andrewes').

Ward, B. (ed.), *Saint Anselm, Prayers and Meditations*. Penguin, Harmondsworth, 1973, p. 201.

Whyte, A. *Lancelot Andrewes and his Private Devotions*. Oliphant, Anderson and Ferrier, London-Edinburgh, 1896, p. 59.

Whyte, p. 57.

2
GEORGE HERBERT
1593–1633

This is what love really is: not that we have loved God, but that
he loves us and sent his Son as a sacrifice to atone for our sins.

1 John 4.10

Steady me, my Herbert. Lay your hands on me.
Thy skill and art, what music would it be?

Micheal O'Siadhail (1998)

The climate of the mind is positively English in its variableness
and instability. Frost, sunshine, hopeless drought and refresh-
ing rains succeed one another with bewildering rapidity.
Herbert is the poet of this inner weather.

Aldous Huxley (1932)

There are many ways to arrive, other than through his biography, on the doorstep of George Herbert's rectory. There are his
poems. Then there is what we know of him through what we
have heard and read, particularly in *The Life of Mr George
Herbert* by Isaak Walton, and, on a broader canvas, how he
stands in relation to the seventeenth century. Yet even before
all that, we have got to realize that he was a man, and a poet,
and later a priest, who felt very much as we feel today, and
people have always felt, living inside this sort of body, and this
sort of mind, and with hopes and fears and desires which move
us beyond ourselves, some sort of belief in things greater than
ourselves. Yet there is a particular element in Herbert which
relates to his love of things Christian, and of things of the
Church. Coleridge puts it like this, scribbled in the margin of
his copy of Herbert's poems:

G. Herbert is a true poet ... the merits of whose poems will
never be felt without a sympathy with the mind and character of the man. To appreciate this volume it is not enough
that the reader possesses a cultivated judgement, classical
taste or even poetic sensibility – unless he be likewise a

51

CHRISTIAN, and both a zealous and an orthodox, both a devout and a devotional, Christian. But even this will not quite suffice. He must be an affectionate and dutiful child of the Church, and from habit, conviction and a constitutional predisposition to ceremoniousness, in piety as in sources of formality. For religion is the element in which he lives, and the region in which he moves. (Coleridge, ed. Whalley, 1984)

George Herbert was born in Montgomery, in 1593. When he was 12, his father having died, he moved with his mother, Magdalen Herbert, to London, where he attended Westminster School. He grew up to be a cultivated, intellectual disciple of the Renaissance. That meant his schooling would have made him versatile in the classical languages and in rhetoric. It is possible that the former Dean of Westminster, Lancelot Andrewes, on his return visits to London, would have met Herbert at Westminster School. Knowledge, a grasp of the way that the world and the heavens worked, was food and drink to the young George Herbert. In the world at large, with a successful merchant economy, and the winning of wars in the Elizabethan era, and the colonization of America, horizons were opening up on every side.

Herbert went from Westminster to Trinity College, Cambridge in 1609, and after his time as an undergraduate, he stayed on to fulfil the more public role of Orator. This meant that he had to give effusive speeches in Latin on the visits of royalty and other dignitaries. It was surely the proximity of Newmarket that allowed Herbert to dally with the culture of the court and of the King, James I. Nearby to Cambridge was Downham, the residence of the Bishops of Ely when they needed to attend directly to their diocese. Lancelot Andrewes was Bishop of Ely while Herbert was at Cambridge and it is highly likely that Andrewes encouraged Herbert in his vocation to the Christian ministry, and in the love of God and of the saintly life, which were to flower in those few short years in his parish at Bemerton. (See the Interlude letter from Herbert to Andrewes, p. 44, 45)

Poetry was an integral part of Herbert's life from quite early on. As an undergraduate at Trinity College he announced his self-conscious resistance to the secular world, particularly with regard to love poetry which was all the rage at the time. He wrote to his mother, who was by all accounts, including John Donne's, a greater influence on her son than anyone else. Herbert wrote:

> I fear the heat of my late Ague hath dried up those springs, by which Scholars say, the Muses use to take up their habitations. However, I need not their help, to reprove the vanity of those many love-poems, that are daily writ and consecrated to Venus; nor to bewail that so few are writ, that look towards God and heaven. For my own part, my meaning (dear Mother) is in these sonnets, to declare my resolution to be, that my poor Abilities in poetry, shall be all, and ever consecrated to God's glory. New Year 1609/10.

There was always a cross-bias in Herbert's involvement in the heady worlds of university and court. He was known as something of a dandy and had a love of fine clothes. The contemporary exaltation of human love, the consecration to Venus, was in the ascendant, and among the poems of that era were Shakespeare's *Sonnets*, first published in 1609, the year that Herbert wrote the letter to his mother. The cross-bias in Herbert's life was his smouldering love for God, and his commitment to ambition and worldly pleasures. It was in the tension between worldly honours and the discipleship of the humble Christ that the poems were forged. Listen to the cross-bias in this poem:

Bitter-Sweet

Ah my dear angry Lord,
Since thou dost love, yet strike;
Cast down, yet help afford;
Sure I will do the like.

I will complain, yet praise;
I will bewail, approve:
And all my sour-sweet days
I will lament, and love.

The hidden years

When Herbert eventually left Cambridge in the summer of 1624, aged 31, he went away for a while, and no one quite knows where. He resurfaces at the end of 1625, having been ordained to a prebendal stall in Lincoln Cathedral, with Leighton Bromswold as a parish, but with no legal requirement to reside or minister there. On the surface this was a classic turnabout, courtier turned curate. We have the poems from that period, and they tell us a lot. They are full of self-doubt, anger, despair, and hanging over everything was the cloud of ill-health. They reflect a 'dark night of the soul' to match any of any period of religious consciousness. Perhaps we need look no further than someone who has taken Christ for his teacher and his example, to explain the strenuous process of becoming a disciple.

Over a period of time, longer than these dark years, a picture was emerging in Herbert's mind, of the nature of God's pattern in this world, and of his place in it. He had committed himself to the priesthood in an established Church with a long tradition, which had in Herbert's time been undergoing huge changes. Mirroring the Renaissance in its explosion of human self-consciousness, human endeavour, learning, and the growth of scientific knowledge, was a reformation in the Church. This meant a shift of power, and a conflict of temperaments and theologies, so severe that it erupted in the Civil War. Herbert was dead by the outbreak of the Civil War, but he was well aware of the battle lines that were marshalling themselves into position.

Ordination

It was with all this surging around in his mind and in the world of the day, that Herbert sufficiently recovered health to contemplate marriage, and admission to the priesthood, as his mother had always desired. The offer of the parish of Bemerton was accepted. Some think it was with the persuasion of King Charles I, and William Laud, with the added incentive of Bemerton's proximity to Wilton House, home of the Pembrokes, but F. E. Hutchinson in his edition of the poems is sceptical about this. Herbert was instituted at Salisbury on 26 April 1630, and so began a three-year incumbency which, through his writings, has become one of the most famous recorded periods of ministry in the Church of England. It is to his poems, and his prose work concerning the nature of the priestly ministry, that we turn for the essence of his spirituality.

When Herbert knew that he was dying, he gathered all his poems together, those of struggle, the ones that represented his transition period into ordination, and those which seem to be completely reconciled to God. All of these he placed quite carefully so that by their order, they were able to reflect on one another, and also to show a progression through the Church's year, and through a theological library of subjects, architectural, legal, theological, all under the heading of *The Temple*. He sent them with a message to his friend Nicholas Ferrar. Ferrar had set up an extended family community at Little Gidding, near Cambridge. Herbert was at Bemerton, close to Salisbury. With the book of poems went this message, recorded in Isaak Walton's *Life*:

> Sir, I pray deliver this little book to my dear brother Ferrar, and tell him he shall find in it a picture of the many spiritual conflicts that have passed betwixt God and my soul, before I could subject mine to the will of Jesus my Master: in whose service I have now found perfect freedom. Desire him to read it; and then, if he can think it may turn to the advantage of any dejected poor soul, let it be made public; if not let him burn it: for I and it are less than the least of God's mercies.

The manuscript had a title, *The Temple. Sacred Poems and Private Ejaculations*. It also had a quotation from Psalm 29: 'In his Temple doth every man speak of his honour.' The poems were organized like a temple. The temple is a building in which are placed four structures or themes: 'The Church Porch', 'Superliminare' or 'threshold', 'The Church', and 'The Church Militant'. Having read Herbert's poems, usually as single poems with no real reference to each other, there has never been an occasion to see how the structure of the whole illumines the individual poems. That is a great loss, because then we do not see the driving force of Herbert's mind as, at the end, he seeks to order both his private and his public thoughts. Take

55

the poem 'Mary Magdalene', for example. It comes towards the end of the poems, reflecting the actions of Mary Magdalene at the time of Jesus' resurrection. Around that poem are bunched others which interact among themselves, 'Bitter-Sweet', 'The Glance', 'The Twenty-third Psalm', 'The Odour', 'The Rose', and 'The Banquet'.

There is a more profound progression, however, which runs counter to Herbert's own order, and that is the progression from struggle, through a transition period, into reconciliation with God. An example of a poem from each of these three periods will be used to look more deeply into the way Herbert feels about his relationship with God and how he expresses this in what we could describe as a mystical way.

He died in 1633, at the age of 40, leaving behind his wife, Jane, his nieces, and a bundle of poems, and an odour of sanctity which remains fresh to this day:

> For when *My Master*, which alone is sweet,
>   And ev'n in my unworthiness pleasing,
>   Shall call and meet,
>   *My servant*, as thee not displeasing,
> That call is but the breathing of the sweet.
>
> This breathing would with gains by sweet'ning me
>   (As sweet things traffic when they meet)
>   Return to thee.
>   And so this new commerce and sweet
> Should all my life employ and busy me.
>   ('The Odour' (ll. 21–30), 2 Corinthians 2)

The impetus to minister

We can talk about all sorts of things, but one of the most important things in the Christian faith, which Herbert teaches us about, is love. I cannot really imagine being committed to anything for very long if my heart was not in it, without in some way, falling in love with it. Duty has its place, law has its place, sleep has its place, but love is the real mover. Love shifts the stars, as Dante put it, and it has certainly shifted me over the years. I could not conceive of having committed myself to a life's work in the ministry of the Church without love being the reason in the first place, and as it has gone on, allowing love to rekindle the spark. All the things that have gone right through my life, through the heart, mind, soul, and strength, have been matters of love.

Yet we need to be sure what that 'love' consists of; because it would be easy to assume, in today's climate, that it means infatuation, or just sex, or a romantic feeling, which lasts no longer than a picnic on a summer's day. The love that Herbert writes about, and what he would have understood by the word, from the Christian teaching he absorbed, would have been firmly based on the idea that love is something which comes from God, and has been shown us most vividly and instructively in the life of Jesus.

> Immortal love, author of this great frame,
>   Sprung from that beauty which can never fade . . .
>
> 'Love (1)'

This was a life of commitment to the will of God, as it was understood by Jesus in his life of prayer, teaching, healing, and his ministry to the troubled and the sinner. It was also a commitment to the world and the place where he was set, and the people he lived among. Herbert's poems 'Love (1)' and 'Love (2)' set the shallowness of romance against the love that 'wrought our deliverance from th'infernal pit'.

I would not put too much weight on the coincidence that Herbert's ministry in Bemerton was exactly the same length of time as his Lord's ministry in Palestine, a short three years. What that fact does do, is remind us that for both, their ministry was rooted in the locality, and the Christian ideal of love was tested for both, by its commitment to the problems and opportunities of the people they lived among. For both, love was made perfect in weakness, and wore the habit of peace, gentleness, kindness, self-control, and, yes, joy. We get a picture of Herbert from Isaak Walton's *Life* of someone who immensely enjoyed music, singing, playing instruments, writing poetry, reading, having his nieces to live with him in the rectory at Bemerton, and walking along the river Avon, which ran along at the bottom of his garden, to Salisbury.

The tradition of 'love'

Love is no new experience, arising in the Christian tradition without any roots further back. It reaches at least as far as the commands of God to the Israelites: 'You must love the Lord your God with all your heart and with all your soul, and with all your strength' (Deuteronomy 6.5; Luke 10.27). The word 'love' in the Hebrew of the Deuteronomy passage covers a lot of ground. It can mean human love for an object, love of son and daughter, man's love to woman, woman's love for man, slave to master, inferior to superior, to neighbour, particularly the stranger, friend to friend, food, drink, husbandry, length of life, sleep, knowledge, and Jerusalem. But what was it like for the Hebrew to love God?

First of all to love God was a commandment. There was no leaving love to chance. It was to love God as the only God, to love God as the one God in a world where there were many gods, many objects of desire, which could become their sole and all consuming desire. The love of God was a particularly pure, directed affection, and obedience to the source of salvation, the giver and author of all good things. Love towards God gave them hope and freedom, and the acceptance that came from right behaviour, and the wisdom to know what that right behaviour was.

> Immortal Heat, O let thy greater flame
>   Attract the lesser to it; let those fires,
>   Which shall consume the world, first make it tame;
> And kindle in our hearts such true desires,
> As may consume our lusts, and make thee way.
>
> 'Love (2)'

A whole-life love

Love was also for the Hebrew something that should grip the whole of life, not just the eyrie of the mind, or the sweatshop of the bowels, or the prayerful soul, or the rose-tinted and perfumed heart, but all of these things, combined into one powerful energized whole, available in such a unified way as to direct its beam on the doing of God's will:

[R]epeat [the commands to love God and neighbour] to your children, and speak of them both indoors and out of doors, when you lie down and when you get up. Bind them as a sign on your hand and wear them as a pendant on your forehead; write them on the doorposts of your houses and on your gates. (Deuteronomy 6.7f)

This love of God, through the keeping of the commandments, was a whole-life business, both as an individual, and in community. Love was the dynamism that kept the covenant.

Jesus imbibes the great tradition of love

We see a great depth of tradition and experience in the Hebrew idea of love. The religious life into which Jesus was born was rich in the tradition of it. It was a word and notion that was constantly on faithful Hebrew lips; but I suspect that as often as it was on the lips of Jesus, there was the process going on in his mind which caused him to say, 'What does this love demand of me?' When we consider what force directed the life of George Herbert, we can see that it was unconditional love from outside himself which had such a great impact. It came, we assume, in the dark days when he was mourning the loss of close friends, when he had left Cambridge and all its securities, where he was appreciated for his skills and worldly learning. The power of his youth had gone underground in the cold grip of winter. Into those dark days was shone a light of love which was unconditional, unwarranted, God-given, and it wore the human face of Jesus his Lord.

The Glance

When first thy sweet and gracious eye
Vouchsafed ev'n in the midst of youth and night
To look upon me, who before did lie
    Welt'ring in sin;
I felt a sug'red strange delight,
Passing all cordials made by any art,
Bedew, embalm, and overrun my heart,
    And take it in.

Since that time many a bitter storm
My soul hath felt, ev'n able to destroy,
Had the malicious and ill-meaning harm
  His swing and sway:
 But still thy sweet original joy,
Sprung from thine eye, did work within my soul,
And surging griefs, when they grew bold, control,
  And got the day.

If thy first glance so powerful be,
A mirth but opened and sealed up again;
What wonders shall we feel, when we shall see
  Thy full-eyed love!
 When thou shalt look us out of pain,
And one aspect of thine spend in delight
More than a thousand suns disburse in light,
  In heav'n above.

Love in Herbert's poetry

This is the love that Herbert speaks of, and knows intimately. It does not, however, with Herbert, float free. It is tied into the framework of intense human experience, but it also refers outwards to the understanding of the sacrificial love of Christ made real for us in the cross and also in the banquet of love, the Eucharist. The symbols of the love of God receiving us into his home are eating and drinking. These are activities at the very centre of our ordinary human experience, and with love as with so many of the 'mystical' experiences we are to deal with here, it is a case of the ordinary revealing the secrets of heaven.

Who knows not Love, let him assay
And taste that juice, which on the cross a pike
Did set again abroach; then let him say
 If ever he did taste the like.
Love is that liquour sweet and most divine,
Which my God feels as blood; but I, as wine.

          'The Agonie'

This is the point. It is love of God in Christ Jesus which makes the difference, does the changing, allows the transformations, and makes the connections between bread and wine, cross and communion, and both these sets, with suffering and joy.

It is interesting to me that Herbert places the experience of Christian love in the Eucharist. The weekly communion which can easily become so routine, and is in fact such a mundane and practical thing, is also the thing that is most happily referred to by the spiritual writers of the period as 'the holy mysteries'. Anglican spirituality is tied by its roots to the earth of the regular sacrament. There, in the experience of the Church, the divine and human meet. Christ becomes a reality among us. In it we are taken by the hand to heaven.

The spirituality of the everyday

So often with the spiritual sensibility there are the two poles of the earthly and the heavenly. They come in many guises: the temporal and the spiritual, the human and the divine, the particular and the universal, the one and the many, the Son of Man and the Son of God. They remain poles apart until something joins them, and that something, in the writing of Herbert, is love. There is a collision of opposites, and the sparks fly. The more extreme the poles, the more profound the collision, and the more intense the love. Love joins these opposites. Love is the junction box that makes the impossible join, possible. Bread becomes body, wine becomes blood, God becomes human and humanity is drawn up into participation in God. For the poet, these paradoxical truths become woven into the language, and the rhythm of the language, and show the Anglican genius for pointing to the truth without being specific:

Which my God feels as blood, but I as wine.

One stage further than just a simple joining, is the insight that what has been joined has also remained distinct, felt as blood by God, but felt as wine by us. The blood and the wine are both the same looked at in one way, and distinct when looked at another way. God feels a true suffering on the cross in Jesus Christ, and by us, this is experienced in the spiritual refreshment of wine.

I imagine that the platonic divisions between appearance and reality caused the images such as love, light, and the word, to take such a prominent place in Christian writing. If our thinking and perceiving are one-dimensional then there is no creative tension, or movement, or need for the image. It is either all image, or all reality. There is no passing from one side to another, no looking through glass, but simply looking at glass. Herbert saw the beyond in the here and now, and in the here and now, participated in the glory of God.

Examples

The Collar

I struck the board, and cried, No more.
        I will abroad.
   What? shall I ever sigh and pine?
My lines and life are free; free as the road,
    Loose as the wind, as large as store.
      Shall I be still in suit?
   Have I no harvest but a thorn
   To let me blood, and not restore
   What I have lost with cordial fruit?
      Sure there was wine
Before my sighs did dry it: there was corn
    Before my tears did drown it.
   Is the year only lost to me?
    Have I no bays to crown it?
No flowers, no garlands gay? all blasted?
      All wasted?
   Not so, my heart: but there is fruit,
     And thou hast hands.
   Recover all thy sigh-blown age
On double pleasures: leave thy cold dispute
Of what is fit, and not. Forsake thy cage,
     Thy rope of sands,
Which petty thoughts have made, and made to thee
   Good cable, to enforce and draw,
     And be thy law,
   While thou didst wink and wouldst not see.
     Away; take heed:
     I will abroad.
Call in thy deaths head there; tie up thy fears.
     He that forbears
    To suit and serve his need,
     Deserves his load.
But as I raved and grew more fierce and wild
     At every word,
Me thoughts I heard one calling, *Child*:
    And I replied, *My Lord*.

The mystic way of coalescing the worldly, and the heavenly, in one creative vision, was not without its problems for Herbert. The effort and the discipline of life, that was involved in pursuing this way, was intense, and was in conflict with the apparent freedom of a life lived according to his own will and not God's. We know it was a struggle for Herbert to lay down the life of a successful orator and courtier, and the intense anguish and frustration of this process is captured in this poem, 'The Collar'.

A 'collar' was a word used to express discipline, and 'to slip the collar' was often used figuratively. Preachers would use the word of the restraint imposed by conscience. The way of dying with Christ, in order to be raised with Christ, which has its most dramatic representation in baptism, can also be experienced in the events of daily life. Perhaps Herbert saw the way of life that his contemporaries were enjoying, and was envious. They had no similar sense of restraint, and were not touched by the disciplines of Christ, nor did they seem to be going through the process of inward transformation necessary, as St Paul puts it, to die to self that they might live for righteousness. Or as the Gospel words of Jesus say, 'Those who save their life will lose it, and those who lose their life for my sake will find it.'

There is a strong element of self-dramatization in this poem. It is powerful, visually and experientially, we can see and hear clearly what is happening, and we can feel the mood. Words of thraldom and servitude abound: 'load', 'cage', 'rope', 'cable', 'tie up'; and terms of barrenness, 'drown', 'blasted', 'sigh', are set vividly against words of freedom and enjoyment such as 'large as store', 'cordial fruit', 'flowers, garlands'. Putting ourselves alongside the way of the world, we might assume that escape and freedom were very good things, but that, as Herbert discovered before us, was not to be the case.

The dramatic resolution of the poem in the last two lines, to mirror the laying out of the dramatic tension in the first line, come with a wonderful calm and serenity. All is resolved in obedience:

> Me thoughts I heard one calling, *Child*:
> And I replied, *My Lord*.

Some might consider reverting to childhood as a means of resolution to be a backward step. What had been the value of all of Herbert's mature experience? Does God not want learning and skill? Not, apparently, before he desires the childlike obedience that allows entrance to the Kingdom of Heaven. To see as a child again involves the painful journey of negation, and the stripping away of adult assumptions about power and freedom such as are described in 'My lines and life are free; free as the road'. True freedom does not lie along that particular road.

It was a discovery that Herbert's near contemporary, St John of the Cross, was also making. St John of the Cross (1542–91) is well known for his writings about 'the dark night of the soul'. Put simply, he shared with Herbert the gospel insight, that until our wills are put alongside the will of God, all our individual strivings are worthless. We will discover that God's binding us to his will can take the form of negation, and a denial of our own selves. A 'no' to this world's delights is replaced by a 'yes' to the supreme delights of God's Kingdom.

The Elixir

Teach me, my God and King,
in all things thee to see,
And what I do in anything,
to do it as for thee:

Not rudely, as a beast,
To run into an action;
But still to make thee prepossessed,
And give it his perfection.

A man that looks on glass,
On it may stay his eye;
Or if he pleaseth, through it pass,
And then the heav'n espy.

All may of thee partake:
Nothing can be so mean,
Which with his tincture (for thy sake)
Will not grow bright and clean.

A servant with this clause
Makes drudgery divine:
Who sweeps a room, as for thy laws,
Makes that and th'action fine.

65

This is the famous stone
That turneth all to gold:
For that which God doth touch and own
Cannot for less be told.

In Herbert's poem 'The Elixir', better known as the hymn 'Teach me, my God and King', this sense of the two worlds, the here and the beyond, are contrasted, and eventually brought into a unity. The window at first seems to divide the worlds. For those who are unable to see through it, the window is a barrier, but for those who look through to the beyond, they can see the glory of God. There is a further stage, and that is when God shines his light through that same window into the ordinary, humdrum world of housekeeping, and 'makes drudgery divine'. God touches, and makes his own, the routine matters of daily life, and by his 'touch', his 'tincture', his 'stone', turns everything to gold.

When we read poetry, we are in a world of image and metaphor, and that has to be embraced, and enjoyed, and entered into, with faith that it is God's way too. Metaphor is allowable. It is alright. To talk of God's coinage as gold, his love as golden, is our way of saying his love is the most precious thing we can imagine. God revealed himself through a human image, Jesus Christ himself.

In his prose work *A Priest to the Temple*, Herbert describes God's love as being very near to us, even in our creatureliness and sin. Parson Herbert in his parish comes across people who doubt that God loves them. Either they cannot believe that God would love such an ordinary person as they, or they feel too sinful to be lovable. They have done too much wrong. Herbert realizes by dint of a deep if not lengthy pastoral experience, and a knowledge of what is in a person, that what those people who feel unlovable need, is the gift of God's grace. Herbert puts it beautifully in his *Country Parson*:

If the parson sees them nearer desperation than Atheism; not so much doubting a God, as that he is theirs; then he dives unto the boundless ocean of God's love, and the unspeakable riches of his loving kindness.

66

If they feel themselves sinners, says Herbert, they must remember that:

> ... as sinful, God must much more love them; because notwithstanding his infinite hate of sin, his love overcame that hate ... gave them love for love, even the son of his love out of his bosom of love.

And if they felt too creaturely, inadequate, or we might say unworthy, he reminds us that God loves his creatures; and

> no perfect Artist ever yet hated his own work.

Love (3)

Love bade me welcome; yet my soul drew back,
    Guilty of dust and sin.
But quick-eyed Love, observing me grow slack
    From my first entrance in,
Drew nearer to me, sweetly questioning,
    If I lacked anything.

'A guest', I answered, 'worthy to be here.'
    Love said, 'You shall be he.'
'I, the unkind, ungrateful? Ah, my dear,
    I cannot look on thee.'
Love took my hand, and smiling did reply,
    'Who made the eyes but I?'

'Truth, Lord, but I have marred them; let my shame
    Go where it doth deserve.'
'And know you not', says Love, 'who bore the blame?'
    'My dear, then I will serve.'
'You must sit down', says Love, 'and taste my meat.'
    So I did sit and eat.

The overturning of our sense of inadequacy by the grace and love of God is most famously expressed in this poem. Herbert, or whoever edited the poems, placed it significantly, at the conclusion of the collection, as a summary of the whole, a summary of Herbert's life.

Herbert had been an occasional member of the travelling court of James I. He had been Public Orator at the University of Cambridge. He was one of the 'glitterati' of his age, but this was all put behind him when he became a priest in the temple of God. His turning to his particular vocation as priest was a culmination of his growing sense of humility, and of his knowing himself to be in need of the love and grace of God. He came to know that any love he might have, or need for himself in loving others, came, in the first place, from God.

Why might we call this poem mystical? When Vaughan Williams completed his settings of five of Herbert's poems in 1911, he entitled them 'Five Mystical Songs'. In the setting of 'Love (3)' Vaughan Williams adds the edenic key of E in the intoning of the *Sacrum Convivium* as the poem moves towards its climax in the heavenly banquet, the Eucharist, or the meal that Jesus shared with the two disciples at Emmaus. An ordinary invitation to a meal is invested with profound implications for us all. We too are unworthy, as the Prayer of Humble Access puts it, 'we are not worthy so much as to gather up the crumbs under your table', and yet love overrules our inadequacy. Love takes the initiative, sweeps us into the banquet, casting aside all the fearful echoes of forgotten wedding garments. The sinful eyes, the shame, the 'dust and sin' are all healed, with a touch, 'Love took my hand'. Here is the 'Song of Songs' transposed into a banquet for all, and love will brook no excuse. This love, God's love, is overwhelming. We do not know properly how to love, and we need to be taught:

> Come my Joy, my Love, my Heart:
> Such a Joy as none can move:
> Such a Love as none can part:
> Such a Heart as joys in love.

> 'The Call'

God teaches us about love in the hospitality of the Eucharist. There the Church retells the deeds of love that God did in Christ. In the Eucharist we declare our inadequacy and know God's 'quick-eyed love', lighting upon us in forgiveness, where we taste and eat. This is ordinary courtesy, couched in English monosyllables, but we read a text between the lines and sense an extraordinary, mystical love that takes us up, and sets us in the Kingdom of Heaven.

Interlude
Magdalen Herbert and John Donne

To Mrs Magdalen Herbert: of St Mary Magdalen

Her of your name, whose fair inheritance
   Bethina was, and jointure Magdalo:
An active faith so highly did advance,
   That once she knew, more than the Church did know,
The Resurrection; so much good there is
   Delivered of her, that some Fathers be
Loth to believe one woman could do this;
   But, think these Magdalens were two or three.
Increase their number, Lady, and their fame:
   To their devotion, add your innocence;
Take so much of th'example, as of the name;
   The latter half; and in some recompense
That they did harbour Christ himself, a guest,
   Harbour these hymns, to his dear name addressed. J. D.

Magdalen Herbert (d. 1627) was the mother of George Herbert
(1593–1633). She was then married to her first husband,
Richard Herbert, of Montgomery Castle. In 1608 she married
Sir John Danvers, an intelligent and wealthy young man not
quite half her age. John Donne was extremely fond of her, and
held her in high respect, and an account of their relationship is
found in Isaak Walton's *Life of Mr George Herbert*.

Magdalen, now Lady Danvers, put her eldest son, Edward,
into The Queen's College, Oxford, and provided him a fit tutor,
and stayed with him in Oxford for four years, and it was there
that she met John Donne. Donne immortalized Magdalen in
his poem, 'The Autumnal Beauty':

   No spring nor summer beauty has such grace,
   As I have seen in an autumnal face.

Isaak Walton continues the story:

This amity, begun at this time and place, was not an amity
that polluted their souls; but an amity made up of a chain of
suitable inclinations and virtues; an amity like that of St

69

Chrysostom's to his dear and virtuous Olympias; whom in his letters he calls his Saint; or an amity, indeed, more like that of Saint Jerome to his Paula; whose affection to her was such, that he turned poet in his old age, and then made her epitaph . . .

And this amity betwixt her and Mr Donne was begun in a happy time for him, he being then near to the fortieth year of his age [in 1611, which was some years before Donne entered into sacred orders, and when George Herbert was 18 and at Cambridge], a time when his necessities needed a daily supply for the support of his wife, seven children and a family. And in this time she proved one of his most bountiful benefactors; and he as grateful an acknowledger of it. You may take one testimony of what I have said of these two worthy persons, from this following letter and sonnet:

"MADAM,

"Your favours to me are everywhere; I use them, and have them. I enjoy them at London, and leave them there; and yet I find them at Mitcham. Such riddles as these become things inexpressible; and such is your goodness. I was almost sorry to find your servant here this day, because I was loth to have any witness of my not coming home last night, and indeed of my coming this morning. But my not coming was excusable, because earnest business detained me; and my coming this day is by the example of your St Mary Magdalen, who rose early upon Sunday, to seek that which she loved most; and so did I. And from her and myself, I return such thanks as are due to one, to whom we owe all the good opinion that they whom we need most have of us. By this messenger, and on this good day, I commit the enclosed holy hymns and sonnets (which for the matter, not the workmanship, have yet escaped the fire) to your judgement, and to your protection too, if you think them worthy of it; and I have appointed this enclosed sonnet to usher them to your happy hand.

"Your unworthiest servant, unless your accepting him to be so have mended him,

"Mitcham, July 11, 1607.   Jo. Donne."'

A further insight into this relationship between John Donne and Magdalen, the mother of George Herbert, lies in the funeral sermon that Donne preached, at Chelsea, on 1 July 1627. Two sections of it will give you the flavour. The first section is a 'consideration of her person':

> God gave her such a comeliness, as, though she were not proud of it, yet she was so content with it, as not to go about to mend it, by any Art. And for her attire ... it was never sumptuous, never sordid; but was always agreeable to her quality, and agreeable to her company; such as she might, and such, as others, such as she was, did wear. For in such things of indifferency in themselves, many times, a singularity may be a little worse, than a fellowship in that, which is not altogether so good. It may be worse, nay, it may be a worse pride, to wear worse things, than others do. Her rule was mediocrity.

The other is the conclusion of the sermon, and describes Magdalen in the manner of the commentators of the Song of Songs. It also introduces us to Donne's views on death, and how closely tied in they are with love, love of the person, and love of the God who has the power to save, and bring to eternal life.

> ... when all we, shall have been mellowed in the earth, many years, or changed in the air, in the twinkling of an eye, (God knows which) that body upon which you tread now, that body which now, whilst I speak, is mouldering, and crumbling into less, and less dust, and so hath some motion, though no life, that body, which was the tabernacle of a holy soul, and a temple of the holy Ghost, that body that was eyes to the blind, and hands, and feet to the lame, whilst it lived, and being dead, is so still, by having been so lively an example, to teach others, to be so, that body at last, shall have her last expectation satisfied, and dwell bodily, with that righteousness, in these new heavens, and new earth, for ever, and ever, and ever, and infinite, and super-infinite evers. We end all, with the valediction of the Spouse to Christ: His left hand is under my head, and his right embraces me, was the Spouse's valediction, and good night to Christ then, when she laid herself down to sleep in the

strength of his mandrakes, and in the power of his spices, as it is expressed there; that is, in the influence of his mercies ...

Therefore, I charge you, o ye daughters of Jerusalem, wake her not, wake her not, with any half calumnies, with any whisperings; But if you will wake her, wake her and keep her awake with an active imitation, of her moral, and her holy virtues. That so her example working upon you, and the number of God's saints, being, sooner, by this blessed example, fulfilled, we may all meet, and meet quickly in that kingdom, which hers, and our Saviour, hath purchased for us all, with the inestimable price, of his incorruptible blood. To which glorious Son of God ... (*Donne's Sermons*, 1919)

Editions

The standard edition of Herbert's works is Hutchinson, F. E., *The Works of George Herbert*, Oxford University Press, 1941.

The poems quoted here are from Herbert, G., *The Complete English Poems*, ed. J. Tobin, Penguin Books, 1991.

References

Coleridge, S. T., *Marginalia 2*. Ed. Whalley, G. Routledge and Kegan Paul, Bollinger James LXXV, Princeton University Press, 1984, p. 1034.

Donne, J., *Sermons*. Selected Passages with an Essay by Logan Pearsall Smith, Clarendon Press, Oxford, 1919, pp. 35–36.

Huxley, A., *Texts and Pretexts*. Chatto and Windus, New York, 1932, p. 13.

O'Siadhail, M., 'Trinity College Chapel, Cambridge', in *Our Double Time*. Bloodaxe Books, 1998, p. 68.

3

JOHN DONNE
1571–1631

> All the way to heaven is heaven.
>
> Donne, *Sermons* (1919)

In 1911, the artist Stanley Spencer was lent a book by Jacques Raverat. It was a copy of Donne's *Sermons*. Spencer was painting pictures which were quite revolutionary for their day, and in reading Donne he found someone who fed the mystical element within him. He read:

> But as my soul, as soon as it is out of my body, is in heaven, and does not stay for the possession of heaven, nor for the fruition of God, till it be ascended through air, and fire, and moon, and sun, and planets, and firmament, to that place which we conceive to be heaven, but without a thousandth part of a minutes stop, as soon as it issues, is in a glorious light, which is heaven (for all the way to heaven is heaven).

Reading that final phrase, he rolled it round his visual mind, and then set to work on the picture, 'John Donne Arriving in Heaven'. We would be excused for thinking heaven was a section of Widbrook Common, but that's the point. For Spencer, and for Donne, walking along the road, and turning the head, was looking into heaven.

It is a mysterious painting without much of the exuberant, scintillating glory of Donne's vision, nor with the fleshy humanity of Spencer's later work, but how gratifying that one of our major artists should be touched and influenced by the mystical writing of John Donne, and celebrate his arrival in heaven, in the evening tones and hues of rural Berkshire.

A footnote to this footnote comes in the very beginning of Rupert Brooke's 1913 essay on Donne, written for *The Nation*. He wrote, 'One of the most remarkable of the English pictures in the recent Post-Impressionist exhibition depicts "John Donne Arriving in Heaven". "I don't know who John Donne

75

is," a sturdy member of the public was lately heard to remark in front of it, "but he seems to be getting there." Unconsciously, he summed up Donne's recent history. Of all the great English poets, his name is least known beyond "literary" circles; but he is certainly getting there' (Hassall, 1956).

John Donne is more the contemporary of Andrewes than any of the other writers assembled here. He was born in 1571, and his early life is well known for its high living. He was born into a Roman Catholic family, his mother being the sister of the Jesuit missionary, Jasper Heywood, and a granddaughter of Sir Thomas More. He entered Hart Hall, Oxford, in 1584 and possibly studied after this at Cambridge, or perhaps abroad. The journey of his life until 1615, at the age of 43, when King James persuaded him to be ordained, was a heady mixture of author, politician, lawyer and penurious husband.

He was supported in his poetic and philosophical life by a group of friends, among whom he distributed his poems. Only two of these were poets, Ben Jonson and Everard Gilpin, the satirist. The others were members of the young, literary, middle-class, intellectual elite, who, like Donne himself, were to become the leading professional men of their time. There was Sir Henry Wotton, later Ambassador to Venice and Provost of Eton; John Hoskyns MP, Judge, Sergeant at Law; Sir Richard Baker MP, High Sheriff of Oxfordshire; Christopher Brook, who became a leading lawyer; and Donne's closest friend, Sir Henry Goodyere, soldier, courtier and patron of the arts.

In 1598 Donne became private secretary to the Lord Keeper, Sir Thomas Egerton, a post from which he was dismissed four years later owing to his secret marriage to Ann More, his master's wife's niece. Despite the apparently footloose way of life this short biography suggests, his religious views were much in his mind.

In the popular mind there are two Donnes. There is Jack Donne of the first half of his life, the Donne who produced the love poetry, and John Donne, Dean of St Paul's, who produced the great religious poems, but there are themes which bind these two halves closely together. One is the sense of deep, if erratic, feeling. You really sense that Donne experienced the highs and lows, and all that goes between, in the way of human emotions. He pushed the boundaries of human feeling to the limits. He must have been an exciting, if unnerving, person to know. He was a sociable person who depended on his friends for intellectual stimulation and also, it has to be said, for advancement in the social and court life of the time. If feeling is one thing that ties the two halves of Donne's life together, intellectual curiosity is another. His mind was well stored with the latest scientific discoveries and humanistic learning, with the sense of travel and different cultures; of astronomy and science and mathematics. He picked from all these the images he needed to girder his poems with the necessary intellectual strength. In his penurious period after his marriage in 1601 he found employment in 'controversial' writing, and in 1610 wrote the *Pseudo-Martyr* to persuade Catholics that they might take the Oath of Allegiance. In the next year he wrote a witty satire on the Jesuits, *Ignatius his Conclave*. Around this period, he composed, but did not publish, *Biathanatos*, a casuistic discussion and defence of suicide.

Coming across the poems at school there were parts of the book which included long poems which looked, and on reading were, very difficult. Someone once said that the poems of Donne were like the peace of God, 'they pass all understanding'. The poems appealed to the intellectuals because they needed a good deal of teasing out. You have to hold quite a lot in your mind at once, and I sensed on first reading them that a different worldview from 1950s suburbia was behind the inner thrust of the poems. Strange words like 'hydroptique' and 'mandrake', 'spheare' and 'confitures' and 'valediction'. I was unaware in the 1950s of the tide of support for the poetry of Donne that had built up over the early years of the century. An important year was the publication of Herbert Grierson's *Metaphysical Poetry from Donne to Butler* (1921) which T. S. Eliot reviewed in an essay that became the manifesto of the cause for 'metaphysical' poetry. Metaphysical was the brand name of poets such as Donne and Herbert who managed to tie together the mind and the heart, intellect and feeling in their poems, and used a daring and innovative sense of rhythm and use of words, to evoke in the very sound of the poems the struggle or the argument, or the growth in the relationship, that the poem was describing.

77

T. S. Eliot described it like this:

Donne instead of pursuing the meaning of the idea letting it flow into the usual sequence of thought, arrests it, in order to extract every possible ounce of the emotion suspended in it. To such ideas of Donne's therefore there is a certain opacity of feeling; they are not simple significance and directions. In their asserting the idea Donne often succeeds in bringing to light curious aspects and connections which would not otherwise be visible; he infuses, as it were, the dose of bismuth which makes the position of the intestine apparent on the X-ray screen. (Eliot, 1993)

The years 1607 to 1610 proved to be a time of spiritual crisis for Donne. He was 35 and his religious thoughts and emotions at that time are charted in the *Holy Sonnets*. There is much discussion on the dating of these poems. Helen Gardner in *Divine Poems* dates six of the sonnets between February and August 1609 and most of them shortly afterwards. The 19 'Holy Sonnets' explore a soul in transition, raw and open wounds, questionings, self-doubt, but there are also poems of tremendous confidence, as if Donne was trying out all his different religious voices. These are the extremes:

> Oh my black soul! Now thou art summoned
> By sickness, death's herald, and champion;
> Thou art like a pilgrim, which abroad hath done
> Treason, and durst not turn to whence he is fled . . .
>
> *(Holy Sonnets* 4, 1–4)

and with the image of himself as of a fortress needing to be stormed, or 'usurp't' by God, he writes this:

> Batter my heart, three-person'd God: for, you
> As yet but knock, breathe, shine and seek to mend;
> That I may rise, and stand, o'erthrow me, and bend
> Your force, to break, blow, burn and make me new.
>
> *(Holy Sonnets* 14, 1–4)

In the middle of this emotional turmoil there are secure points to hold on to: one is the loving forgiveness of Christ:

Mark in my heart, o soul . . .
The picture of Christ crucified, and tell
Whether that countenance can thee afright,
. . . can that tongue adjudge thee unto hell,
Which prayed forgiveness for his foes' fierce spite?

Holy Sonnets 13, 2–3, 7–8

Death, despair and sin hold him in an iron grip. What will release him from them, but a stronger magnet, Grace, which will 'like adamant draw mine iron heart' (*Holy Sonnets* 1, 13, 14)? Christ in the incarnation, in his coming to earth as man, is able to disarm Satan, and defeat death:

'Twas much, that man was made like God before,
But, that God should be made like man, much more.

(*Holy Sonnets* 15, 13, 14)

and back to that poem I mentioned in the introduction, the one in the clothy grey-green Penguin book, 'Death be not proud' (*Holy Sonnets* 10). This is Donne at his most assured and defiant. There is a strong dependence on the ideas of St Paul:

One short sleep past, we wake eternally,
And death shall be no more, death thou shalt die.

Holy Sonnets 10, 13, 14

'Everything that we know of Donne indicates that, during the years from his marriage in 1601 down through the time of his ordination in 1615, he was engaged in the most fervent and painful self-analysis, directed toward the problem of his vocation' (Martz, 1954).

It is Louis Martz who has helped us place Donne's poetry in the tradition of St Ignatius of Loyola's *Spiritual Exercises*, in which those anticipating a deeper involvement in the ministry of the church, or an 'election' as Ignatius calls it, are encouraged to meditate on the very themes which we find uppermost in the *Holy Sonnets*: the love of God, death, and the day of judgement.

Yet if there was one theme which epitomizes Donne's concerns, it is the subject of death. This is not a subject which the present century is at all comfortable with. That is partly because it has lost its faith in any life beyond death, partly due

79

to its ability to cure illnesses which in the seventeenth century brought death to so many. We may say, thank goodness for that, and certainly the morbidity that was engendered by a constant attention to death is something we might be glad to be released from. Yet death is a reality for all, it is a major feature of being human, and therefore it is not surprising that it is so common in the writings of poets, and religious people. For Donne it was a constant subject for his sermons and poems.

Donne did not write just about one aspect of death. He saw it in all its various ways. It was the death of his wife Ann which must have been one of great influencing factors in Donne's own thinking about death. They were married in 1602. She gave birth to 11 children, three of whom died in infancy. It was her 12th child's stillbirth that was the cause of Ann's death in 1617. Donne, in his famous sermon 'Death's Duell', writes of the tragedy of stillbirth:

> The womb which should be the house of life, becomes death itself, if God leaves us there, that which God threatens so often, the shutting of the womb, is not so heavy, not so dis-comfortable a curse in the first, as in the latter shutting, nor in the shutting of barrenness, as in the shutting of weakness, when children are come to the birth, and there is not strength to bring forth.

> The death of his wife marked a turning point in Donne's life; it deepened his sense of religious vocation, and produced some-thing much closer to a conversion than the feelings which had prompted him to enter the Church. Until her death all Donne's deepest emotional experiences seem to have been as-sociated with her; after her loss, his emotions concentrated themselves on the divine image and the activities connected with his sacred calling. Commentators have long been aware of the increased intensity of religious feeling expressed by Donne after 1617, and he himself was conscious of the change. It was shown in the enrichment of his preaching and in his deepened sense of Christian truth. (Bold, 1970)

Isaak Walton in his life of Dr John Donne put it like this:

> Immediately after his return from Cambridge his wife died, leaving him a man of a narrow unsettled estate and (having

buried five) the careful father of seven children then living, to whom he gave a voluntary assurance, never to bring them under the subjection of a stepmother: which promise he kept most faithfully, burying with his tears all his earthly joys in his most dear and deserving wife's grave, and betook himself to a most retired and solitary life.

In this retiredness, which was often from the sight of his dearest friends, he became *crucified to the world*, and all those vanities, those imaginary pleasures, that are daily acted on that restless stage; and they were as perfectly crucified to him. (Walton, n.d.)

Donne meditated on death and saw it in its many weathers. In the early love poems, like 'The Good-Morrow', death is kept at bay by love. As the biblical book the Song of Songs puts it, 'Love is strong as death', and Donne wrote, 'If our two deaths be one, or, thou Love so alike, that none so slacken, none can die.'

The well-known quotation 'never send to know for whom the bell tolls, it tolls for thee' is about the mutuality of life as a human being on earth. We share in a common humanity and therefore one person's death is, in a way, part of our experience too, 'Each man's death diminishes me'. Death is the common lot, and it rushes up to meet us, 'I run to death and death meets me as fast' (*Holy Sonnets* 1), but in Donne's mind it is his sin which makes death such a terror, and the grace of God in releasing him from the burden of his sin, also releases him from the fear of death. Sickness is 'death's herald and champion', a little death which reminds us of the greater death to come. It is quite a simple and straightforward philosophy, or theology. Death is a reality. It is a moment of judgement in which the righteous and the unrighteous will both be given their just rewards, and to benefit from the joys of heaven we need to call on the love of God to free us from our sins.

It is a theology which today has come to seem too simplistic. The divine division between righteous and unrighteous, the idea of a supernatural judge, and a real devil, the concept of a life after death, all seem rather remote from our own 'live-for-ever, do-what-you-like', humanist culture. It would be easy to put Donne aside and box him into a seventeenth-century corner. Why, then, do his poems still resonate? Underlying his theology, his thoughts about the nature of God and human death, there is a close relationship with God. It is an experienced and felt theology. You really do feel that Donne sensed the power of death, and the consequent responsibilities that that imposes, and even if we cannot accept the severity of the distinctions, we can certainly share the fears, and the reality of the experience of what it is to be faced by this great, and obvious mystery:

> This is my play's last scene, here heavens appoint
> My pilgrimage's last mile: and my race
> Idly, yet quickly run, hath this last pace,
> My span's last inch, my minute's latest point,
> And gluttonous death, will instantly unjoint
> My body, and soul, and I shall sleep a space,
> But my 'ever-waking part shall see that face,
> Whose fear already shakes my every joint ...

Holy Sonnets 6

Donne's 'ever-waking part' is his soul. That's a splendid way of putting it. The soul, the *anima*, the part of us that God could permanently animate, keep alive and awake. If we do not surround it in so many wrappings and obliterate it altogether, we 'shall see that face', the face of God. It is the soul that will 'take flight'. If in the course of our lives we can keep the soul, as God would wish, alive by the forgiveness of sins and the pursuit of the love of God and our fellow human beings, then that will be released from the 'earth-borne body', and leave the world, the flesh and the devil, way behind.

It is these thoughts that Donne meditated on in a hundred different ways with one telling image after another, in a rhythm and style which hold us to his thought, while being exhilarated by the feeling which drives the thought. I have not said enough about the one who makes our fear of death unnecessary, Christ himself. The whole apparatus of fear surrounding death focused on the devil, hell, punishment, separation, pain, finds its release in the cross, and the infinite mercy and love of God shown in Christ's death.

82

Father, part of his double interest
Unto thy kingdom, thy Son gives to me,
His jointure in the knotty Trinity
He keeps, and gives me his death's conquest.
This Lamb, whose death, with life the world hath blessed,
Was from the world's beginning slain, and he
Hath made two wills, which with the legacy
Of his and thy kingdom, do thy sons invest.
Yet such are thy laws, that men argue yet
Whether a man those statutes can fulfil;
None doth, but thy all-healing grace and Spirit
Revive again what law and letter kill.
Thy law's abridgement, and thy last command
Is all but love; oh let that last will stand!

Holy Sonnets 16

It is Donne's way, as it is with all our writers here, to find images which bring alive to the reader the force of this gift of Christ the Son to us. The image in *Holy Sonnet* 16 is 'two wills'. To understand it we have for a while to enter into the legal aspect of death, into the world of the Inns of Court with which Donne was so familiar. In this case we are dealing with the two wills, made by God, from the beginning of the world, the old and the new wills. The legacy made in the wills is invested by his followers, us if you like. The laws surrounding God's first will make it difficult for the inheritors to fulfil their obligations, as in the old covenant, but the second will is all about love.

A vivid picture of Donne's attitude to death comes in the description of his own preparation for it, and in what was to be his final sermon, 'a kind of new ritual expressing the doctrines of his religion', as his biographer R. C. Bold put it. Attitudes to death were very different in the seventeenth century from today, and what we might think of as macabre would be seen in those days as a suitable preparation for death's mysteries. The skull on the table, the *memento mori*, were very good ways of holding mortality before their eyes, and of increasing their dependence on the grace of God. Preparation was of the essence. Life itself was a preparation for death, 'for this whole world is but a universal churchyard'.

Donne's dramatic temperament led him, as Walton

describes, to pose for his own memorial. Donne with a fixed plan in his mind, first caused a wooden urn to be carried and then procured a plank the size of his body. Then, when charcoal fires had been lit in his study, he took off his clothes, and had his shroud put on him, with knots tied at head and foot. With the shroud turned back to show his face, and his face towards the east, he stood on the urn with closed eyes while an artist sketched his figure life-size on the wooden plank. This drawing Donne kept at his bedside to remind him of what he was soon to be.

Before this sketch was made, a copy of which was to become the frontispiece for the printing of his final sermon, he preached that same sermon at Whitehall on Friday 25 February 1631.

> When to the amazement of some beholders he appeared in the pulpit, many of them thought he presented himself, not to preach mortification by a living voice: but, mortality by a decayed body and a dying face ... after some faint pauses in his zealous prayer, his strong desires enabled his weak body to discharge his memory of his preconceived meditations, which were of dying: the text being, 'To God the Lord belong the issues from death'. Many that then saw his tears, and heard his faint and hollow voice, professing they thought the Text prophetically chosen, and that Dr Donne had preached his own Funeral Sermon.

The description of Donne's final days, and then hours, by Isaak Walton is a classic piece of writing, both reverent and matter of fact. It places the idea of a serious preparation for death at the heart of the matter. Death was at its most dangerous when it came unexpectedly, or violently, and so without due warning and without an earnest and holy preparation. Donne was not going to let chance have its way.

> And now he was so happy as to have nothing to do but die; to do which, he stood in need of no longer time; for he had studied it long, and to so happy a perfection ... He lay fifteen days earnestly expecting his hourly change; and in the last hour of his last day, as his body melted away, and vapoured into spirit, his soul having, I verily believe, some revelation of the beatified vision, he said, 'I were miserable

84

if I might not die': and after those words closed many periods of his faint breathing by saying often, 'Thy kingdom come, thy will be done'. His speech, which had long been his ready and faithful servant, left him not till the last minute of his life, and forsook him not to serve another master ... but died before him ... Being speechless, and seeing heaven by that illumination by which he saw it, he did, as St Stephen, 'look steadfastly into it, till he saw the Son of Man standing at the right hand of God' his Father; and being satisfied with their blessed sight, as his soul ascended and his last breath departed from him, he closed his own eyes, and then disposed his hands and body into such a posture, as required not the least alteration by those who came to shroud him.

He died on 31 March 1631, aged 60.

Examples

A Hymn to Christ, at the Author's last going into Germany

In what torn ship soever I embark,
That ship shall be my emblem of thy Ark;
What sea soever swallow me, that flood
Shall be to me an emblem of thy blood;
Though thou with clouds of anger do disguise
Thy face; yet through that mask I know those eyes,
    Which though they turn away sometimes,
        They never will despise.

I sacrifice this Island unto thee,
And all whom I loved there, and who loved me;
When I have put our seas 'twixt them and me,
Put thou thy sea betwixt my sins and thee.
As the trees sap doth seek the root below
In winter, in my winter now I go,
    Where none but thee, th'eternal root
        Of true love I may know.

Nor thou nor thy religion dost control,
The amorousness of an harmonious Soul,
But thou wouldst have that love thyself: as thou
Art jealous, Lord, so I am jealous now,
Thou lov'st not, till from loving more, thou free
My soul: who ever gives, takes liberty:
    O, if thou car'st not whom I love
        Alas, thou lov'st not me.

Seal then this bill of my Divorce to All,
On whom those fainter beams of love did fall;
Marry those loves, which in youth scattered be
On fame, wit, hopes (false mistresses) to thee.
Churches are best for prayer, that have least light:
    To see God only, I go out of sight:
        And to 'scape stormy days, I choose
           An everlasting night.

Donne is off to Germany. He was setting out by boat in 1619, as a member of Viscount Doncaster's train in the embassy, and they are to go via Brussels. It was a slightly less extravagant embassy than usual, owing to the recent death of the Queen, but it was a distinguished enough group, that required the services of Donne as a chaplain. Donne seems to have been in low spirits at the time, and wrote to some of his friends that he may not be in contact with them. He took solemn leave of his congregation with a sermon at Lincoln's Inn:

> ... if I never meet you again till we have all passed the gate of death, yet in the gates of heaven, I may meet you all, and there to my Saviour and your Saviour, that which he said to his Father and our Father, 'Of those whom thou hast given me, have I not lost one'. Remember me thus, you that stay in this kingdom of peace where no sword is drawn, but the sword of Justice, and I shall remember you in those Kingdoms, where ambition on one side, and a necessary defence from unjust persecution on the other side hath drawn many swords; and Christ Jesus remember us all in his kingdom, to which, though we must sail through a sea, it is the sea of his blood, where no soul suffers shipwreck: though we must be blown with strange winds, with sighs and groans for our sins, yet it is the Spirit of God that blows all this wind, and shall blow away all contrary winds of diffidence or distrust in God's mercy; where we shall be all soldiers of one army, the Lord of Hosts, and children of one choir, the God of harmony of consent ... (Smith, 1919)

On 4 May 1619 the embassy was ready to set out, but the winds were unfavourable and the shipping was not available at Gravesend. There was time for Donne to nurse his low spirits, and to write a poem, 'A Hymn to Christ, at the Author's last going into Germany'. The title is a combination of the sublime and the ordinary, with a sense of mortality in that decisive word 'last'.

The poem works by the use of 'emblems'. Emblems are simply pictures of deeper realities. Emblem books were popular at the time. Donne sees everything to do with this journey as an emblem of the deeper reality of Christ's saving love. Setting the tangible, worldly things like sea and human love as emblems of deeper realities is very much the hallmark of the 'metaphysical' poets.

87

The message of the poem is a simple one. God is all. The world, and all that is in it, is an emblem of a particular aspect of God's totality. Since God is God, that puts everything else in the shade, and of less value, until it is seen in its emblematic nature, as a pointer to God's salvation. So the 'torn ship' is Noah's 'ark', the North Sea is Christ's blood, the clouds (remember it was the weather held them in Gravesend) a disguise which hides God's face (see Exodus 33.20), but despite his hiddenness, God 'never will despise'.

The journey away from England is an emblem of the putting away of sin, and of Christ's sacrifice which put a distance between humanity and its sin. Donne's journey to Germany is an emblem of the discovery of the eternal root of God's love, 'true love' as he calls it. This 'true love' gives Donne the opening for a more tortuous description of the difference between his love and the love of God.

The third verse is the most difficult to understand. Human love, which is summed up in verse 4 by 'false mistresses', is a poor emblem of God's love. The inadequacy of the emblem is that God's love would subsume all other loves. God's love makes human love seem inadequate, purposeless. 'Jealousy', which is a common aspect of human love, is an emblem of the divine 'jealousy' which we see in the Old Testament, in which God is often a 'jealous' God. By this jealousy, he longs for people to experience the love which he can give. Donne seems to be asking God to take liberties with him, and driven by a purified 'jealousy' to have a real care and concern that the object of Donne's love should be God, and God alone. This is a thought which Donne uses in his poem 'A Hymn to God the Father':

> I have a sin of fear, that when I have spun
>   My last thread, I shall perish on the shore;
> But swear by thy self, that at my death thy son
>   Shall shine as he shines now, and heretofore;
>   And, having done that, Thou hast done,
>   I fear no more.

So Donne divorces all his former loves for the sake of God. He goes into the darkness and the storm of the voyage (they embarked eventually from Margate, several days late). The darkness blocks out all other concerns, other than the one thing

88

necessary to salvation, which is the contemplation of the love of God in Christ.

This way of seeing everything as an image of the character and presence of God, is also an acknowledgement of the supremacy of God. God is in everything, but most significantly in the person of Christ, for Christ is the true image, the image of the invisible God, and the cross his most powerful emblem. Donne returns again and again to the emblem of the cross:

> Who can deny me power, and liberty
> To stretch mine arms, and mine own cross to be?
> Swim and at every stroke, thou art thy cross;
> The mast and yard make one, where seas do toss;
> Look down, thou spiest out crosses in small things;
> Look up, thou seest birds raised on crossed wings . . .
>
> 'The Cross'

Such use of images has a way of allowing the whole world to be interpenetrated with divine truth. The flying birds are both visual images of the cross, and also, by being that, become imbued with the power of the cross itself. Rather than demeaning humanity by the power of the image, it is raised to the one whose image it bears.

This interpretation of the image and the divine does not only occur with people, animals, and objects, but also with words. The particular word 'cross' is an image of the thing it describes. It contains a power comparable to the object it describes, and the word, too, can take on multiple meanings which cross-refer to each other. Donne's own name is a word he often plays with, so that its various meanings are made clearer: 'And, having done that, Thou hast done.' Donne is saying that when he dies and Christ can shine his forgiveness and love upon him, then God the Father will certainly have done his work, and will have Donne as well, and Donne will 'fear no more'.

There is an element of play in this. Puns, playing on words, were a very common part of the way language was used in Tudor and Elizabethan times. It had its humorous and ironic side. Shakespeare used it to full advantage in his plays. It is a sort of verbal acrobatics, but by harnessing the technique to his purposes in the *Divine Poems,* Donne makes language the plastic, malleable instrument he needs to tie various levels of reality together, and to say more than one thing at a time. It could be that in a moment of history when science was beginning to eliminate the power and presence of God, by discovering a one-dimensional world which was without a God, Donne used language to maintain the closest possible connection between human realities and divine ones, so that within the one dimension of language, God and man, so to speak, could remain distinct, but intimate, realities.

Good Friday, 1613. Riding Westward

Let man's Soul be a Sphere, and then, in this,
The intelligence that moves, devotion is,
And as the other Spheres, by being grown
Subject to foreign motions, lose their own,
And being by others hurried every day,   5
Scarce in a year their natural form obey:
Pleasure or business, so, our souls admit
For their first mover, and are whirled by it.
Hence is't, that I am carried towards the West
This day, when my soul's form bends toward the East.   10
There I should see a Sun, by rising set,
And by that setting endless day beget;
But that Christ on this Cross, did rise and fall,
Sin had eternally benighted all.
Yet dare I'almost be glad, I do not see   15
That spectacle of too much weight for me.
Who sees God's face, that is self life, must die;
What a death were it then to see God die?
It made his own lieutenant Nature shrink,
It made his footstool crack, and the sun wink.   20
Could I behold those hands which span the Poles,
And turn all spheres at once, pierced with those holes?
Could I behold that endless height which is
Zenith to us, and our antipodes,
Humbled below us? or that blood which is   25
The seat of all our souls, if not of his,
Made dirt of dust, or that flesh which was worn
By God, for his apparel, ragg'd and torn?

90

If on these things I durst not look, durst I
Upon his miserable mother cast mine eye, 30
Who was God's partner here, and furnished thus
Half of that sacrifice, which ransomed us?
Though these things, as I ride, be from mine eye,
They are present yet unto my memory,
For that looks towards them; and thou look'st towards
   me, 35
O Saviour, as thou hang'st upon the tree;
I turn my back to thee, but to receive
Corrections, till thy mercies bid thee leave.
O think me worth thine anger, punish me,
Burn off my rusts, and my deformity, 40
Restore thine image, so much, by thy grace,
That thou mayst know me, and I'll turn my face.

The situation described at the beginning of this poem seems a very modern one. There is rush, hurry, busyness, and our souls are distracted, fixed on everything except God. This is as true in our time, more so, I should think, than in 1613, when Donne was travelling westward, on the very day he would have liked to be concentrating on the passion of Christ, for which we traditionally turn east, and be able to feed on that for his prayers and meditations.

To lead us into the poem, Donne draws a cosmographical picture, 'Let man's soul be a sphere'. We have to imagine these spherical objects floating about, but generated by some motor, some force which moves them. Unfortunately, there are competing strengths of force, and each sphere affects the other, and there is general chaos. Donne says this is like the soul. The 'devotion' that moves the soul is distracted, and pulled out of its natural course, by pleasure, or business, and is 'whirled by it'. Vaughan has a whole poem devoted to the problem, called 'Distraction', which has the lines:

> The world
> Is full of voices; Man is called, and hurled
>   By each, he answers all,
>   Knows every note, and call,
>   Hence, still
> Fresh dotage tempts, or old usurps his will.

So our good intentions to pray are too easily put aside by more pressing things. This is a very familiar experience. What is fresh is Donne's image, or emblem, for it. He locates this experience in the journey he was making from the east to the west of the country. He was travelling westwards from Mitcham to Montgomery Castle, to visit George Herbert's brother, Edward.

In his fertile imagination, the comparison of the sun rising and setting to Christ's dying and rising, rings all sorts of bells for Donne, and kindles all sorts of resonances. We need to enter that imaginative world to make much sense of the poem. The end point is that Christ, although imaged by the sun, outdoes it, takes over from it, and provides the light for those who are stuck at the point of eternal night. Interest in the spheres, in astronomy, and in the scientific basis of the world, from which Donne delights to draw many of his images, led in the matter of half a century, to the discoveries of Sir Isaac Newton (1642–1727). Donne stands at the crossroads between the ancient and the modern world, as do all of our writers, but none so acutely conscious of the straddling as Donne. His very rhythms echo the struggle of the search to use the new learning for the old truths:

> On a huge hill,
> Cragged, and steep, Truth stands, and he that will
> Reach her, about must, and about must go . . .
>
> 'Satire 3'

At line 15, there is a distinct change of mood:

> Yet dare I'almost be glad, I do not see
> That spectacle of too much weight for me.

Donne makes something positive out of what could have been just a negative, disappointing experience. Lines 17–28 are based on the text in Exodus 33.20, 'My face you cannot see, for no mortal may see me and live', which is picked up, in a more general way, in 2 Corinthians 3. As the biblical text tells us, Jesus, as Son of God, also cannot be looked at without death being the consequence, and this is exactly what happened to the natural world at the time of the crucifixion. The sun went dark, and the earth cracked. Donne, therefore, could not possibly have looked on Jesus:

92

Could I behold those hands which span the Poles,
And turn all spheres at once, pierced with those holes?

(lines 21–22)

He cannot look directly at Christ, but he can look with his memory, and since Donne's memory is focusing on Jesus, and Jesus can engage with that, then there is both a looking and a response, on this Good Friday 1613.

In line 36 we return to this tremendous sense of physicality in Donne:

O Saviour, as thou hang'st upon the tree;
I turn my back to thee . . .

This seems the height of discourtesy, until we see the reason for it, which is 'to receive correction', and allow that correction to continue 'till thy mercies bid thee leave'. This 'correction' is probably the traditional practice of 'the discipline' in which the penitent inflicted his own punishment with a small whip, sometimes made of sharp, iron pieces. Yet there is another way in which the restoration of the image of Christ in Donne can be effected other than self-mortification, and that is by God's grace:

Restore thine image, so much, by thy grace,
That thou mayst know me, and I'll turn my face.

(lines 41–42)

The connections between the inner spirit of Donne, and his outer body (back, eyes, face), and then again between the body of Christ and the universe, and then between each of these sets of relations, build up a whole range of creative patterns and echoes. In the wonderful opening phrase 'Let man's soul be a sphere' there is a movement from the miniature to the larger scale, as when 'Christ on this cross did rise and fall', and in doing so reflected, and in the end, took precedence over, the sun's activities. God's hands 'span the poles', Donne's journey moves from one side of England to another. There is movement in the poem as much in the verse as in the subject, and there is a resolution as in 1 Corinthians 13, when man and God meet face to face: 'That thou mayst know me, and I'll turn my face'.

Death's Duel

This Sermon was titled 'Death's Duel, or a Consolation to the Soul, against the dying Life, and living Death of the Body'. It was delivered at Whitehall before Charles I in the beginning of Lent 1630.

But for us that die now and sleep in the state of the dead, we must all pass this posthume death, this death after death, nay this death after burial, this dissolution after dissolution, this death of corruption and putrifaction, of vermiculation and incineration, of dissolution and dispersion in and from the grave, when these bodies that have been the children of royal parents, and the parents of royal children, must say with Job, 'Corruption thou art my father, and to the worm thou art my mother and my sister'. Miserable riddle, when the same worm must be both father and mother to my own mother and sister, beget and bear that worm which is all that miserable penury; when my mouth shall be filled with dust, and the worm shall feed, and feed sweetly upon me, when the ambitious man shall have no satisfaction, if the poorest alive tread upon him, nor the poorest receive any contentment in being made equal to princes, for they shall be equal but in dust. One dieth at his full strength, being wholly at ease and in quiet, and another dies in the bitterness of his soul, and never eats with pleasure, but they lie down alike in the dust, and the worm covers them; in Job and in Isaiah it covers them and is spread under them, the worm is spread under thee, and the worm covers thee. There's the mats and the carpets that lie under, and there's the state and the canopy, that hangs over the greatest of the sons of men; even those bodies that were the temples of the Holy Ghost, come to this dilapidation, to ruin, to rubbish, to dust, even the Israel of the Lord, and Jacob himself hath no other specification, no other denomination, but that worm of Jacob. Truly the consideration of this posthume death, this death after burial, that after God (with whom are the issues of death) hath delivered me from the death of the womb, by bringing me into the world, and from the manifold deaths of the world, by laying me in the grave, I must die again in an incineration of this flesh, and in a dispersion of that dust. That that monarch, who spread over many nations alive, must in his dust lie in a corner of that sheet of lead, and there, but so long as that lead will last, and that private and retired man, that thought himself his own for ever, and never came forth, must in his dust of the grave be published, and (such are the revolutions of the graves) be mingled with the dust of every highway, and of every dunghill, and swallowed in every puddle and pond: This is the most inglorious and contemptible vilification, the most deadly and peremptory nullification of man that we can consider . . .

The moment of death is one thing, the decomposition that follows is another. Donne calls it a 'posthume death'. This death is a common humiliation for everyone. The body must disintegrate, or vermiculate. The dictionary, and I needed it here, tells me that 'vermiculate' means 'the fact or condition of being infested with or eaten by worms'. Job says to corruption, 'Thou art my father', and to the worm, 'thou art my mother and my sister' (Job 17.14). No details are spared. Donne seems to relish the details of mortality. Meditation, by means of the Ignatian *Exercises*, with a skull on the desk, on the reality of death and of the pains of hell, will be some of the influences that lie behind this sermon. In addition, there will be Donne's own proximity to death, the deaths of his children, and the ever-present reality of death in the streets, houses, prisons and hospitals of plague-ridden London.

To push the imagination into the realms of 'posthume death' seems excessive to us. It offends our tidy, self-confident, this-worldliness, but Donne pushes his thoughts to the limit, and presses them. It is rather as though he gets carried away with the scene he has set up for himself, and cannot leave it until a new and more exciting idea hoves into view. After his incest through the activity of the worms, comes the levelling of all classes and types of people. Rich and poor, monarch and servant, will all be children of dust. 'Dust thou art, and unto dust shalt thou return', and the worm will be king. It was T. S. Eliot who said: 'About Donne there hangs the shadow of the impure motive; and impure motives lend their aid to a facile success. He is a little of the religious spell-binder, the Reverend

Billy Sunday of his time, the flesh-creeper, the sorcerer of emotional orgy' (Eliot, 1926).

Donne uses his texts to advantage. We can't really say he is
the first in his school of melodrama. Job and Isaiah provide a
conceit, which works for Donne in a visual, architectural way:
'They shall lie down alike in the dust, and the worms shall cover
them' (Job 21.26 AV), and 'the worm is spread under thee, and
the worms cover thee' (Isaiah 14.11 AV). From which Donne
paints this picture:

> There's the mats and the carpets that lie under, and there's
> the state and the canopy, that hangs over the greatest of the
> sons of men. Even those bodies that were temples of the Holy
> Ghost, come to this dilapidation, to ruin, to rubbish, to
> dust . . .

'Fear not, thou worm of Jacob' (Isaiah 41.14 AV). Yes, fear,
Jacob, because you too are subject to vermiculation, that is
'being eaten by worms'. Even Donne himself knew that there
was no escape from death, nor was there any escape for the
quiet, retiring man, who in time will be 'published', and
'mingled with the dust of every highway, and of every dunghill,
and swallowed in every puddle and pond'.

No one could paint a more vivid picture. Our sensibilities
revolt against it, preferring to have death hidden away from
us. In our own society we can have the luxury of that; in Ausch-
witz, not so, nor in many parts of our war-torn world. Yet
Donne is a man of faith. Preaching, as he is here, on the text
from Psalm 68.20 (AV), 'Unto God the Lord belong the issues
of death', one of his main points is that we have to leave the issue
of death to God, and our faith brings us hope:

> Unto God the Lord belong the issues of death, and by recom-
> pacting this dust into the same body, and reinanimating the
> same body with the same soul, he shall in a blessed and glor-
> ious resurrection give me such an issue from death, but estab-
> lish me into a life that shall last as long as the Lord of life
> himself.

I see my own children's fascination with testing the boundaries.
How much fear can you take, even in a controlled situation?
They want to push the boundaries of reality at funfairs, at

theme parks, and at the cinema, in films and videos, in rock climbing, and in who knows what when I'm not around. Donne, in the controlled situation of a sermon, is allowing his congregation to do the same playing. He is taking them, in their imaginations, further than they are used to going, before the death-ride comes to a stop on the turn of the hourglass. People seem to like practising death in a form where they know things are under control. Donne knew it was soon to be out of his control.

Further on in the sermon, the tone is more moderate. Donne raises the important matter of preparing for death, while our life is still strong, and our minds active. This, surprisingly, involves realizing God's disinterest in death. God never mentions, never seems to consider the bodily, the natural death. However death may come, violent death, or a gentle and preparing sickness, or a frantic fever, 'a gate into heaven I shall have, for from the Lord is the cause of my life, and with God the Lord are the issues of death'.

> I thank him that prays for me when the bell tolls, but I thank him much more that catechises me, or preaches to me, or instructs me how to live. 'Do this and thou shalt live', there's my security, the mouth of the Lord hath said it: but though I do it, yet I shall die too, die a bodily, a natural death. But God never mentions, never seems to consider that death, the bodily, the natural death. God doth not say, live well and thou shalt die well, that is, an easy, a quiet death; but live well here; and thou shalt live well for ever. As the first part of a sentence pieces well with the last, and never respects, never hearkens after the parenthesis that comes between, so doth a good life here flow into an eternal life, without any consideration, what manner of death we die: but whether the gate of my prison be opened with an old key (by a gentle and preparing sickness), or the gate be hewn down by a violent death, or the gate be burnt down by a raging and frantic fever, a gate into heaven I shall have, for from the Lord is the cause of my life, and with God the Lord are the issues of death.

97

Interlude
Henry Vaughan and George Herbert

Henry Vaughan, after lamenting the writings of his youth, and the growing number of books which contain '*oaths*, horrid execrations, and a most gross and studied *filthiness*', complains not only of the printers who print the stuff, but also of those who circulate manuscripts 'when it fails of entertainment at the press'. He continues with a remedy, and the example of George Herbert.

The true remedy lies wholly in their bosoms, who are the gifted persons, by a wise exchange of *vain* and *vicious subjects*, for *divine themes* and *celestial praise*. The *performance* is easy, and were it the most difficult in the world, the *reward* is so glorious, that it infinitely transcends it: for *they that turn many to righteousness, shall shine like the stars for ever and ever:* whence follows this undeniable *inference*, that the *corrupting of many*, being a a contrary *work*, the *recompense* must be so too; and then I know nothing reserved for them, but *the blackness of darkness for ever;* from which (O God!) deliver all penitent and reformed *spirits*!

The first, that with any effectual success attempted a *diversion* of this foul and overflowing *stream*, was the blessed man, Mr *George Herbert*, whose *holy life* and *verse* gained many pious *converts*, (of whom I am the least) and gave the first check to a most flourishing and admired *wit* of his time . . .

It is true indeed, that to give up our thoughts to pious *themes* and *contemplations* (if it be done for piety's sake) is a great *step* towards *perfection;* because it will *refine*, and *dispose* to devotion and sanctity. And further, it will *procure* for us (so easily communicable is that *loving spirit*) some small *prelibation* of those heavenly *refreshments*, which descend but seldom, and then very sparingly, upon *men* of an ordinary or indifferent *holiness;* but he that desires to excel in this kind of *hagiography*, or holy writing, must strive (by all means) for *perfection* and true *holiness*, that a *door may be opened to him in heaven*, Rev. iv 1 and then he will be able to write (with *Hierotheus* and holy *Herbert*) a *true hymn*.

From *The Author's Preface to the Following Hymns*, a preface to the volume *Silex Scintillans*, by Henry Vaughan (1976). The *Preface* concludes with this inscription:

Newton by *Usk*
near *Sketh-rock*
30 September 1654

Editions

POEMS

There are numerous editions of Donne's Poems. The quotations of the poems here are taken from *John Donne, the Complete English Poems*, ed. Smith, A. J., Penguin Classics, 1996.

SERMONS

The most accessible book for reading a selection of Donne's Sermons is Logan Pearsall Smith, *Donne's Sermons, Selected Passages*, Oxford, 1919.

References

Bold, R. C., *John Donne, A Life*. Clarendon Press, Oxford, 1970, p. 328.

Donne, J., *Sermons*. Selected Passages with an Essay by Logan Pearsall Smith, Clarendon Press, Oxford, 1919, p. 218.

Donne, *Sermons*, pp. 32, 33.

Eliot, T. S., 'For Lancelot Andrewes', *Times Literary Supplement*, 23 September 1926, p. 621.

Eliot, T. S., *The Varieties of Metaphysical Poetry, The Clark Lectures*. Ed. Schuchard, R., Faber and Faber, London, 1993, pp. 85–86.

Hassall, C. (ed.), *The Prose of Rupert Brooke*. Sidgwick and Jackson, London, 1956, p. 85.

Martz, L. L., *The Poetry of Meditation*. Yale University Press, Newhaven and London, 1954, pp. 218–19.

Walton, I., *The Life of Dr John Donne*, SPCK, London and New York, 1929, pp. 29–30.

4
HENRY VAUGHAN
1622–95

Behold, Posterity, who I was and what kind of man, lest tomorrow belittle the glory of today. Wales gave me birth, in the place where Father Usk launches down from the windswept mountains to wander in broad valleys.

Henry Vaughan, To Posterity (1976)

These all died in faith . . . and confessed that they were strangers and pilgrims on the earth. For they that say such things declare plainly that they seek a country. And truly, if they had been mindful of that country from whence they came out they might have had opportunity to have returned. But now they desire a better country, that is, an heavenly: wherefore God is not ashamed to be called their God: for he hath prepared for them a city.

Hebrews 11.13–16 (AV)

Why do I want to begin with Vaughan and the night, when he, above all, is a poet of light? Light, of course, depends on darkness, but with Vaughan the night is important because the sort of light he talks about, writes about, and has within his bones, is the light that shines in the darkness. He has drunk deeply from the prologue of St John's Gospel, where the light shines in the darkness, and the darkness has not extinguished it.

Vaughan loved nature, and he particularly loved the night sky with its stars. He loved its sense of being up there, closer to the heavenly realms, and the night was a time when he could feel in touch with God. There were fewer distractions, and the sounds were the sounds of God's creatures which did not jar on the profound silence. A silence, and stillness, and a night sky we now find it very difficult to experience.

His short prose work *The Mount of Olives*, a companion piece to his poem 'The Night', which we shall be looking at in more detail later, begins with a celebration of the night as a time of prayer:

In the primitive church, the saints of God used to rise at midnight to praise the Rock of their salvation with hymns and spiritual songs. In the same manner shouldst thou do now, and contemplate the orders of the stars, and how they all in their several stations praise their Creator. When all the world is asleep, thou shouldst watch, weep, and pray, and propose unto thyself that practice of the Psalmist: 'I am weary of my groaning, every night wash I my bed, and water my couch with tears (Ps. 6.6)'; for as the dew which falls by night is most fructifying, and tempers the heat of the sun, so the tears we shed in the night make the soul fruitful . . . Christ Himself in the daytime taught and preached, but continued all night in prayer, sometimes in a mountain apart, sometimes amongst wild beasts, and sometimes in solitary places.

The Mount of Olives

Vaughan is in some ways the most complex of the writers we are looking at, and the most varied. There is some discussion among contemporary scholars as to whether he is a poet of light, or of darkness. He is both, I'm sure, but whether it is the light emerging from the darkness, or the darkness swamping the light, is difficult to tell. He would, I think, want to distinguish between the night-time, which was resonant for him of the chance to meet God, and the darkness which represents the enemy of light, in a moral way. The darkness is representative of the forces of chaos, and anarchy, and disruption which were all around him in the events of his time. Of all the writers represented here, he was most caught up in the Civil War. Into the crucible of his poetic spirit were poured the light of God's love, the darkness of man's violence and disobedience, and also this half-light of the spiritual world lived in the present, but hinting at the full light beyond. His own time, and his sensitivity to it, expressed in his writings, allows us to share in what is a very similar situation to our own. There is a sadness and a melancholy lurking underneath much of what he writes, which the consolations of the natural world, the hills, the stars, the rivers, strive to heal. The struggles, and the humanity of Vaughan, bring him very close to us.

I want to try and come to Henry Vaughan through this

103

essential contrast in his writings between light and dark. The opposites in creative writing often provide the necessary power to bring about great work, but first some basic biographical details.

Henry Vaughan (1622–96) was educated at Jesus College, Oxford and was the author of many poems, including *Silex Scintillans*, a collection of religious poems. *Silex* means flint, and *Scintillans*, flashing or sparkling. In his title, Vaughan is imagining the sparks that fly when God strikes a person's heart. In the Latin emblem explaining his title page, Vaughan describes the divine power and alludes to both Ezekiel 11.19, 'I will take the stony heart out of their flesh and will give them an heart of flesh' (AV), and to Moses striking the rock and producing water for the Israelites (Exodus 17.1–6).

After two years at Oxford (1638–40), Henry left to study law in London, but was called home in 1642 at the outbreak of the Civil War, in which he served committedly on the royalist side. He was twice married, and though there is no record of a medical degree, he practised medicine at Newtown on the River Usk for most of his life, and wrote and translated medical and medical-alchemical works. He composed and translated various prose works, including essays from Plutarch, a life of Paulinus of Nola, and religious meditations, collected in the book mentioned above, called *Mount of Olives*.

The Mount of Olives had a particular place in the life of Jesus, and Henry Vaughan, a lover of hills as sacred places, found it was very important for him too:

> Sweet, sacred hill! on whose fair brow
> My Saviour sat, shall I allow
>   Language to love
> And idolise some shade, or grove,
> Neglecting thee?

'Mount of Olives'

There may have been a dramatic religious conversion occasioned by the death of his younger brother, William, in 1648, but this was probably just one of many elements that helped to develop his strong religious sense. Another was the influence of the 'blessed man, Mr. George Herbert, whose holy life and

verse gained so many pious converts (of whom I am the least)'
(Preface to *Silex Scintillans*). Vaughan died at the age of 73 in
1695.

With the contrast in Vaughan's life between light and dark, I
want to begin with the darkness. There is much in all these
writers to give us a sense of hope, not least because they all
believe in God, and I imagine that all of them would have
been sympathetic, and helpful, to any who came to them hon-
estly seeking a way through despair or loss of faith. It is with
Vaughan that I feel we can come closest to someone who
would have understood our modern condition, and the darkness that surrounds us in the world, and who would have been
conscious in talking about the love of God of those who find it
difficult to feel any love at all. He was, we remember, a doctor
as well as a poet, and is the only one of our writers who was not
an ordained priest, or if I can put it this way, a professional
theologian. He would have sympathized with those who
experienced darkness.

The Darkness

For many people it is the darkness of their experience which is
uppermost: experiences which are too dark to relate, too hor-
rific to face, too deep to articulate, and yet if we do recognize
them at all, we ask, 'How does that square with the love of
God?' Attending the Crown Court in Winchester, or anywhere,
reading the daily newspaper, we cannot remain immune to
some of the horrendous crimes that come out of the depths of
human cruelty. What darkness! How do we respond to the
searching question, 'Where is God in the dark rooms of child
abuse, torture, and cruelty, or on a wider scale, the famines,
and the wars, and the darkness of the Holocaust?'

Henry Vaughan wrote at a time of intense social upheaval:
the English Civil War. It obviously affected him greatly,
because his Christian belief and practices were under threat,
and it is believed that his brother was killed in the war. The
darkness for him was deeply personal, and it was into his
poems that he poured out his troubled soul, and not only his
poems, his prose writing as well. In this prayer, his inner darkness comes out very strongly:

105

Thou seest, O God, how furious and implacable mine enemies are: they have not only robbed me of that portion and provision which Thou hast graciously given me, but they have also washed their hands in the blood of my friends, my nearest and dearest relatives. (*Mount of Olives*)

Vaughan continues with a plea for help so that he does not feel revengeful: 'Though they persecute me unto death, though they have taken the bread out of the children's mouth, and have made me a desolation; – yet, Lord, give me the grace, and such a measure of charity as may fully forgive them.'

Suffering, and responses to suffering, are universal feelings. How do we cope with them? It sounds a bit weak to say 'we do what we can', but that is probably very near the truth. Very often it is a matter of taking the suffering into our souls, of feeling it, and letting it make wounds in us. We weep and say 'Lord, have mercy on us, sinners'. Others, who can be generous in a financial way, will give financial help. Others will study to understand the motives, the social reasons, and the psychology of evil. What do we do?

The Holocaust

I have a vivid memory of coming out of the Holocaust Museum in Jerusalem, saying to myself, 'Let this feeling of deep respect for the sufferings of others, from now on, inform my attitudes and my words'. How can I be so trivial when so many millions died in the concentration camps, with such huge waste of life? Particularly I was moved by a photograph of a young Jewish mother with a Jewish badge on her coat, and her young son, perhaps six years old, peeping his head out between the buttons of that coat. It was like an icon of the Virgin Mary and the Christ child, and perhaps that is saying more than words could ever say about the relationship of God to suffering.

Evil affects me by making me want to be serious, and to be ready to be solemn for others in their grief, so that we can share in, and be more deeply connected with, the very important matters of life and death. It makes me want to be with God, so that I can learn why things are as they are, why this sort of world is as it is. Why love has to allow its opposite to exist, by reason of the existence of a greater principle of human freedom, which even God has to respect.

The experience of evil makes me want to value the light, the things to do with joy, peace, goodwill, beauty, and truth, when I see them. I then want to acknowledge that they are images of a much greater light, longing to break through if we could only allow it to, or choose it. This greater light, of which our concepts of light are an image, is a reality which, once experienced, can, strangely, in comparison with our own light, be felt as darkness. That is because God, knowing we cannot face the full glare of his light, comes to us as a felt darkness, not the darkness of evil, but as a compassionate shade:

> There is in God (some say)
> A deep, but dazzling darkness; as men here
> Say it is late and dusky, because they
> See not all clear . . .
>
> 'The Night', lines 49–52

The half-light

We move gently and painfully away from the darkness into Vaughan's intermediate half-light, and to help us with this I want to recall a visit I made to the country around Vaughan's home, having hitchhiked and bussed from Worcestershire, and arrived in the Usk Valley towards evening. It was summer and it was one of those amazing experiences of place, when I felt I had come home. Usually careful about dates and times, on this occasion I am muddled about the year and why I was where I was at all, but it was the Usk Valley, and the low sun was shining across the valley 'where roads dip and where roads rise' as T. S. Eliot put it in his poem 'Usk'. I was walking along lanes, I remember, in an almost random way, thinking I could lie down to sleep wherever I was, if need be, and having this enormous sense of goodwill and alrightness, and the river gliding on between fields of cows and sheep. Or, am I remembering the paintings of Samuel Palmer, and imagining myself in one of his golden landscapes, where the natural world is transfigured by the sun which is not only shining on the landscape but shining out from within it? The sheep are so at home they must be shepherded by Christ. Where I slept that night, or where I went the next day, I can no longer remember. It was just a moment of peace on earth and good will to all, and I felt for a while like one of whom Vaughan spoke:

> They are all gone into the world of light!
> . . .
> I see them walking in an air of glory,
> . . .
> O holy hope! and high humility,
>   High as the Heavens above!
> These are your walks, and you have showed them me
>   To kindle my cold love . . .

'They are all gone into the world of light!', lines 1, 10, 13–16

It is a paradox to say that God is both dark and light at the same time. How can that be, except by assuming two realities: God's reality, and our reality? God's perfect light we see and perceive in our limited way. For Vaughan, the perfection of God is reserved for eternity, and this world is a shadow of that perfection.

In the same way, that perfect love has its worldly images and signs, such as for love, there is the touch, the kiss, the washing of wounds, the gaze, the stillness, and the closeness. So the brilliance and perfection of God has for its signs and images, light of all sorts, the stars, the sun, the dawn, and the eyes by which we see light, the candles and beacons with which we shine light for others to see by. Modern images would include electricity and lasers, with all the rich potential they have for linking God the Creator with modern technology and science.

Christ the light

One major image I have not mentioned yet is Christ, the image of God himself, the light, the true light that is in the world. St John is very much attuned to this mystery, and works most creatively with the image of light as the image of God, mediated through Jesus Christ. St John's Gospel, we could say, shines with light. It is in St John's Gospel that Nicodemus visits Christ by night, and for Vaughan this is the most evocative of

108

meetings. He brings together in his poem 'The Night', the shades of day and night in the earthly world, and sets alongside that the realities of the heavenly light and its compassionate shade. By making those connections he leads us to a longing to live in God:

> O for that night! where I in him
> Might live invisible and dim.
>
> 'The Night', lines 53–54

To combat the darkness of human evil and ignorance, we have the light of the lamp that shines into the hearts and minds of the sick or abused. We have the illumination of the mind, and the light we can cast by our human understanding on the problems of the age, and we have the light that shines from Christ into the lives of those who spend time with him, pursuing with him the will of our heavenly Father. Christ, as the light of the world, sheds a light into a darkness:

> When thou dost shine darkness looks white and fair,
> Storms turn to music, clouds to smiles and air:
> Rain gently spends his honey-drops, and pours
> Balm on the cleft earth, milk on grass and flowers.
> Bright pledge of peace and sun-shine!
>
> 'The Rainbow', lines 9–13

Christ's light is like no other, different in amount and quality, different from the natural light, because it has a special moral quality. What do I mean by that? The light that is Christ has a transforming effect on our lives: Vaughan thinks of what effect Christ had on Nicodemus when they met by night:

> Most blest believer he!
> Who in that land of darkness and blind eyes
> Thy long expected healing wings could see,
>   When thou didst rise,
> And what can never more be done,
> Did at mid-night speak with the Sun!
>
> 'The Night', lines 7–12

The light of Christ helps us to know and to want goodness. In that light we hunger and thirst after righteousness, and are distressed by the evil within. That light reveals motives in us, it teaches us about who we really are. It does not just brown the outside, it illuminates the secrets of our hearts. From the light of Christ we are illuminated to proclaim the gospel in our words and actions.

We are mortals. 'We see at present through a glass darkly', and it is Henry Vaughan who describes the environments of religious light. I think I must have come very close to him when I was drifting through the hinterlands of the English-Welsh border one summer holiday between college terms.

Light and shade fill his works, and so do eyes. The light is not always full glare, although the famous line 'They are all gone into the world of light' does suggest that of Vaughan. There is something often holding him back, and the dark side of his experience is explored, as a contrast to the light. This exploration of the light within the darkness is a traditional mystical theme, often traced back to the writings of Dionysius the Areopagite. Vaughan's prayer was often cast in gloom and struggle, and this inevitably made the place where God and the faithful were, that much brighter, in contrast to the gloom he felt himself to be in. He had his eyes, though, looking upwards in prayer to the source of light where the faithful are gathered, and as he looks up he sees the stars, the moon, and the hills, and the rainbow. Ascension Day inevitably supplies him with the subject of ascent, and of upward moving and looking:

> And yet some
> That know to die
> Before death come,
> Walk to the sky
> Even in this life . . .
>
> 'Ascension-Hymn'

Vaughan had the sense of a journey to be embarked on from the below to the above, and that above was another country, as different as light is from the dark, and 'far beyond the stars'.

Let me finish this account of Henry Vaughan in the words of Walter de la Mare:

When Vaughan pines for a 'country far beyond the stars', it would be as vain to argue that this is false or devoted doctrine as to adjure a linnet to be content in a cage. Two weapons he asked for the defeat of the enemy – a living faith, a heart of flesh. In him imagination and faith were at one. The one sets the other burning. He did not turn aside from the ordinary morning to write his poetry. He did not cultivate a beautiful seclusion. His poetry is merely a record of the realest and most intimate things of a workaday life. Its supreme things are never prepared for. They are as intrinsic a part of it as is the sudden all-changing light of greeting in a sensitive face. It is as impossible to discredit such witness as it is impossible to discredit the happiness, or grief, or rapt inklings of a child'. (de la Mare, 1953).

Examples

Regeneration

1

A ward, and still in bonds, one day
    I stole abroad,
It was high-spring, and all the way
    Primrosed and hung with shade;
      Yet it was frost within,   5
        And surly winds
Blasted my infant buds, and sin
    Like clouds eclipsed my mind.

2

Stormed thus, I straight perceived my spring
    Mere stage, and show,   10
My walk a monstrous mountained thing
    Rough cast with rocks, and snow;
      And as a pilgrim's eyes
        Far from relief,
Measures the melancholy sky   15
    Then drops, and rains for grief,

3

So sighed I upwards still; at last
    'Twixt steps, and falls
I reached the pinnacle, where placed
    I found a pair of scales,   20
    I took them up and laid
      In the one late pains,
The other smoke, and pleasures weighed
    But proved the heavier grains;

4

With that, some cried, *Away* straight I   25
    Obeyed, and led
Full east, a fair, fresh field could spy
    Some called it, *Jacob's bed*;
      A virgin-soil, which no
        Rude feet ere trod,   30

112

Where (since he stepped there,) only go
    Prophets, and friends of God.

5
Here, I reposed; but scarce well set,
    A grove descried
Of stately height, whose branches met   35
    And mixed on every side;
    I entered, and once in
        (Amazed to see't,)
Found all was changed, and a new spring
    Did all my senses greet.   40

6
The unthrift Sun shot vital gold
    A thousand pieces,
And heaven its azure did unfold
    Chequered with snowy fleeces,
    The air was all in spice   45
        And every bush
A garland wore; thus fed my eyes
    But all the ear lay hush.

7
Only a little fountain lent
    Some use for ears,   50
And on the dumb shades language spent
    The music of her tears.
    I drew her near, and found
        The cistern full
Of divers stones, some bright, and round   55
    Others ill-shaped, and dull.

8
The first (pray mark,) as quick as light
    Danced through the flood,
But, the last more heavy than the night
    Nailed to the centre stood;   60
    I wondered much, but tired
        At last with thought,
My restless eye that still desired
    As strange an object brought;

9

It was a bank of flowers, where I descried   65
   (Though 'twas mid-day,)
Some fast asleep, other broad-eyed
   And taking in the ray,
   Here musing long, I heard
    A rushing wind   70
Which still increased, but whence it stirred
   No where I could not find;

10

I turned me round, and to each shade
   Dispatched an eye,
To see, if any leaf had made   75
   Least motion, or reply,
   But while I listening sought
    My mind to ease
By knowing, where 'twas, or where not,
   It whispered; *Where I please.*   80

Lord, then said I, *On me one breath,*
And let me die before my death!

One key to this poem lies in its title. 'Regeneration' is a word that is used in the Christian Church for baptism. Baptism is the process of rebirth into Christ, and this poem is an elaborate allegory, a picture story, of a journey into full membership of the Church, the Body of Christ. St Paul describes this in Romans 8.14–15, where he calls the unregenerate state one of slavery, which partly explains the first line of the poem, 'A ward, and still in bonds'.

There are three landscapes hidden in the poem: one is the road between Llansantfraed and Llanhamlach, a walk Vaughan often took, the second is the inner landscape of the poet's mind, and the third is the journey into Christ through baptism. Vaughan goes on a special sort of journey in the first geographical landscape, 'and all the way/ *Primrosed*' (1.4), the second he carries round within himself, and the third he longs for, as the religious route, but sees much of what he loves and lives for blown apart by the Civil War. The journey is set up as a secret one, he 'stole abroad', and his inner feelings are of sin, shame, and dejection. In his poem 'The Night', Vaughan describes another secret event, the meeting of Christ and Nicodemus, where again the main theme is baptism, or regeneration, into the mystical life of Christ. In this poem, 'Regeneration', Vaughan climbs. He reaches the top of a 'pinnacle', and there, surprisingly, and with the shock of a mood change, he finds a pair of scales. On these scales he weighs the respective values of his recent problems against 'smoke and pleasures'. The problems are expected to be heavy, and are light; the 'smoke and pleasures' are expected to be light, but are 'proved the heavier grains' (1.24).

The connection between the scales and the next move is not at all clear. It probably means that since his recent problems are light on the scales, they are not to be worried about, and therefore, released from the burden of them, new ways open up. One new way is to the east, to the biblical land of Jacob's dream, and of a ladder set up from earth to heaven, with the angels ascending and descending on it. This was the place of meeting with God, an awesome place of revelation, and of renewed commitment for Jacob. There Jacob made a vow: 'If God will ... protect me on my journey and give me food to eat and clothes to wear, so that I come back safely to my father's house, then the Lord shall be my God (Genesis 28.20). A journey into discipleship with Christ without attention to the Old Testament heroes and prophets would not be complete, but there is more to the journey than this.

The repose is temporary, because something else catches Vaughan's eye, and that is a grove. The grove is resonant of the classical gods, but also of the nave of a church, and of a place of water, as in baptism. The grove is soaked with a religious light, and there is a fountain there. It is also a place of the Spirit, and in the bowl of the fountain, where the water of baptism and the gift of the Holy Spirit lie, there are a variety of stones, or gifts of the Spirit. The first stone is Adam, and the last is Christ. 'Nailed to the centre stood' (1.60) means the crucified Christ. 'The first ... as quick as light Danced through the flood' (lines 57–58) is Adam in the Garden of Eden, and by analogy, Christ, since Christ was the last Adam.

The 'bank of flowers' (1.65) is the setting for the gift of the Holy Spirit to the apostles, into which Vaughan himself steps, to see

115

what effect the Spirit is having on the 'shades'. 'Shades' is a very important word for Vaughan. He uses it a lot, both to indicate the shade given by the dark leaves, but also to indicate the unregenerate, those who live still untouched by the Spirit of God. Vaughan felt himself to be in need of regeneration. So he confronts the Spirit, only to find that the Spirit has taken the initiative, and addresses him, saying '*Where I please*' (1.80). To this invitation, Vaughan responds with the final words of the poem:

> Lord, then said I, *On me one breath,*
> *And let me die before my death!*

The paradox of dying to self, before one physically dies, is a well known thought in the New Testament: 'Whoever gains his life will lose it; whoever loses his life for my sake will gain it' (Matthew 10.39), and in St Paul's thought, to die with Christ is to rise with him (1 Corinthians 15.22; Romans 14.8). To die to self before our human death is to be, indeed, in the process of regeneration.

Peace

> My soul, there is a country
>   Far beyond the stars,
> Where stands a winged sentry
>   All skilful in the wars,
> There above noise, and danger
>   Sweet peace sits crowned with smiles,
> And one born in a manger
>   Commands the beauteous files,
> He is thy gracious friend,
>   And (O my soul awake!)
> Did in pure love descend
>   To die here for thy sake,
> If thou canst get but thither,
>   There grows the flower of peace,
> The rose that cannot wither,
>   Thy fortress and thy ease;
> Leave then thy foolish ranges;
>   For none can thee secure,
> But one, who never changes,
>   Thy God, thy life, thy cure.

116

You might know this poem as a hymn, 'My soul, there is a country' with a melody by M. Vulpius, and arranged by J. S. Bach; or, as one of the *Songs of Farewell* set to music by Sir C. Hubert Parry. Recall the times. The Civil War is raging, the monarchy is under threat, the Church of England is in ruins. It is suggested that Vaughan was involved in the Civil War, but as a physician not as a combatant, and that he was present at the siege of Beeston Castle. At the time the poem was written, there was certainly no worldly peace, but Vaughan clings on to a deeper peace, the peace that passes all understanding, and is not of this world.

Vaughan talks to his soul. The poem is a dialogue between himself and his soul. For Vaughan, the soul was a very important part of the human character. It was the part that God had specially created, and was formed to be responsive to God if allowed and encouraged. Vaughan addresses his soul and says, 'there is more to life than what we see and hear around us', 'there is a country far beyond the stars'.

Ironically, this poem about peace is full of the images of war, and these images are used powerfully to heighten the sense of peace. In heaven, there is a 'sentry all skilful in the wars'. Christ, the 'one born in a manger commands the beauteous files'. Heaven is a 'fortress'. We are encouraged to 'leave our foolish ranges'. This imagery of war pervades the whole poem, but it is used in the cause of peace, in the same way as the image of the armour is used in Ephesians 6. Heaven is well protected. When the images of peace occur, they are all the more beautiful and peaceful.

What is heaven like? It is 'above noise, and danger' where 'sweet peace sits crowned with smiles'. In the Kingdom of Heaven, Jesus is both commander, and gracious friend:

> He is thy gracious friend,
>   And (O my soul awake!)
> Did in pure love descend
>   To die here for thy sake ...

Heaven is the place where the rose, the flower of peace, is immortal and 'cannot wither'. The cure, and here speaks the doctor, is God himself. He is the 'one who never changes', and Parry in his setting uses this phrase, by repetition, to

117

spiral the words up to heaven, in a most intricate and glorious way.

The Night

John 3.2

Through that pure *Virgin-shrine,*
That sacred veil drawn o'er thy glorious noon
That men might look and live as glow-worms shine,
    And face the moon:
  Wise *Nicodemus* saw such light   5
  As made him know his God by night.

  Most blest believer he!
Who in that land of darkness and blind eyes
Thy long expected healing wings could see,
    When thou didst rise,   10
  And what can never more be done,
  Did at mid-night speak with the Sun!

  O who will tell me, where
He found thee at that dead and silent hour!
What hallowed solitary ground did bear   15
    So rare a flower,
  Within whose sacred leaves did lie
  The fulness of the Deity.

  No mercy-seat of gold,
No dead and dusty *Cherub* nor carved stone,   20
But his own living works did my Lord hold
    And lodge alone;
  Where *trees* and *herbs* did watch and peep
  And wonder, while the *Jews* did sleep.

  Dear night! this world's defeat;   25
The stop to busy fools; care's check and curb;
The day of Spirits; my soul's calm retreat
    Which none disturb!
  Christ's progress, and his prayer time;
  The hours to which high Heaven doth chime.   30

  God's silent searching flight:
When my Lord's head is filled with dew, and all

His locks are wet with the clear drops of night;
   His still, soft call;
  His knocking time; the soul's dumb watch,   35
  When Spirits their fair kindred catch.

    Were all my loud, evil days
Calm and unhaunted as is thy dark Tent,
Whose peace but by some *Angel's* wing or voice
    Is seldom rent;   40
   Then I in Heaven all the long year
   Would keep, and never wander here.

    But living where the sun
Doth all things wake, and where all mix and tire
Themselves and others, I consent and run   45
    To every mire,
  And by this world's ill-guiding light,
  Err more than I can do by night.

    There is in God (some say)
A deep but dazzling darkness; as men here   50
Say it is late and dusky, because they
    See not all clear;
  O for that night! where I in him
  Might live invisible and dim.

Imagine the pure light of God, brighter than the sun. We cannot, easily. It is too bright for the human eyes to stand, and so God has given us the necessary shade to see him by, and that is Christ. Christ softens, filters the bright light of God, reflects it, and that reflected light is as the night is to the day. Light, yet dark. Light, because we know that Christ is the light, and yet that light is dark in comparison with the light of God. Christ in his human form channelled that light for us in a way that we can manage. If we have that gradation of lights clearly in our minds, we can begin to enter into the meaning of this poem. Diagrammatically it looks like this:

Light –	God	–	Sun
Light mediated as dark –	Christ	–	Moon
Human beings –	Glow-worms with light from the moon –		Glow-worms

119

One other point is an historical one. In the fifth century a writer called Dionysius, with the pseudonym the Areopagite (he was taken for the Areopagite of Acts 17.34), wrote his mystical works about God being a 'hid Divinity'. That means that God is hidden in all his fullness from human beings, because humans cannot cope with the full brightness of the deity. So we now see only through a glass darkly, as St Paul put it. We live and trust in 'a cloud of unknowing'. We journey through 'a dark night of the soul', where not to know is an essential state for true knowing, because if we think we know everything, we most certainly do not. God will reveal himself, face to face, in the time to come. In comparison with God's time to come, the here and now is dark, a night-time for the soul. So we know now, paradoxically, by not knowing. It is an idea which has captured the imaginations of many mystics through the centuries, among them the anonymous author of *The Cloud of Unknowing*.

Dionysius writes this in a letter to the monk Gaius:

> Darkness disappears in the light, the more so as there is more light. Knowledge makes unknowing disappear, the more so as there is more knowledge. However, think of this not in terms of deprivation, but rather in terms of transcendence, and then you will be able to say something truer than all truth, namely, that the unknowing regarding God escapes anyone possessing physical light and knowledge of beings. His transcendent darkness remains hidden from all light and concealed from all knowledge. Someone beholding God and understanding what he saw has not actually seen God himself but rather something of his which has being and which is knowable. For he himself solidly transcends mind and being. He is completely unknown and non-existent. He exists beyond being and he is known beyond the mind. And this quite positively complete unknowing is knowledge of him who is above everything that is known. (Pseudo-Dionysius, 1987)

It is against this background of the unknowability of God that Vaughan sets his poem.

Vaughan uses the story in John 3 of Jesus' meeting with Nicodemus by night to give substance to this mystical theology. The

night gives him the ideal setting. John writing his Gospel probably had this in mind too. It was not just by chance that he set a
story of revelation in the night.

> Through that pure *Virgin-shrine*,
> That sacred veil drawn o'er thy glorious noon.

This is Christ, veiling the unsearchable light of God. Christ is
the '*Virgin-shrine*' and 'the sacred veil',

> That men might look and live as glow-worms shine,
> And face the moon . . .

The moon is Christ, and since glow-worms, which in the poem
represent us human beings, draw their light from the moon, so
we draw our light from Christ.

> Wise *Nicodemus* saw such light
> As made him know his God by night.

Nicodemus showed his wisdom by realizing that he could
'know God' through the mediated and comparative darkness
of the moonlight, which is Christ: 'Most blest believer he!'
High praise is given to Nicodemus, because being a Jew, he
would not naturally be expected to recognize the Son of God
in Jesus, or see him as the long-expected Messiah, who comes
with healing in his wings. Yet he does, and at the right time
during Christ's earthly life – a meeting which is denied us. To
call Jesus the sun is a little confusing because in the previous
verse (verse 1), he called him the moon, but I suppose here he
is heightening the glory of Jesus, and contrasting the time of the
meeting, 'the mid-night', with the complete opposite.

'O who will tell me, where he found thee.' Vaughan is interested in places, and where things happen. He is very much an
outdoor poet: in hills, the streams, the plants. He sees Christ as
a rare flower, and is keen to place him in his setting, because
Christ can give a blessing to the place where he is. He sets it up
as a question in verse 3, and answers it in verse 4.

The mercy-seat, and dusty cherubs, and carved stone of the
Temple of Solomon was not the place where Jesus would be
found at night, but among the living works of the creation, on
the Mount of Olives. Here, nature was awake and watching,
and worshipping too. If the world of nature was important for

Vaughan, so was the night-time. In verse 5, Vaughan takes time out to write about the virtues of the night in this lovely verse:

> Dear night! this world's defeat;
> The stop to busy fools; care's check and curb . . .

We can understand '*Christ's* progress' in the way we read about in Mark 1.35: 'And rising very early, going out, he went into a desert place and there he prayed' (AV), and Luke 21.37, 'And in the daytime he was teaching in the Temple; but at night going out he abode in the mount that is called Olivet' (AV). The 'progress' is from the Temple to the place of prayer. At this point, the meeting with Nicodemus slips away from Vaughan's interest and he is overtaken by the tangible and physical sight of Christ at prayer:

> God's silent searching flight:
> When my Lord's head is filled with dew, and all
> His locks are wet with the clear drops of night . . .

Dripping with dew now, but in Gethsemane, before the crucifixion, his brow was dripping with sweat, like drops of blood. Christ's 'still, soft call' is his 'Abba, Father! Thy will be done!' The Father's or the Son's, for we also remember the still, soft voice of God in 1 Kings 19.12. This was Jesus' 'knocking time'.

When George Herbert wrote his poem 'Prayer', and we know Vaughan was greatly influenced by Herbert, he used some very bold images to describe those prayers that came with real force, such as 'engine against the Almighty . . . reversed thunder'. In this verse Vaughan uses the Gospel word of 'knocking', 'knock and it shall be opened unto you'. Christ was knocking at heaven's gate: 'Behold, I stand at the door and knock' (Revelation 3.20, AV).

> . . . the soul's dumb watch,
> When Spirits their fair kindred catch.

Among the ways of praying at night there is silent prayer, 'the dumb watch', a time when the spirits, good and bad, are hovering round. There is a strong resonance here with the Song of Songs 5.2, 'I sleep but my heart waketh: it is the voice of my beloved that knocketh, saying, Open to me, my sister, my love, my dove, my undefiled: for my head is filled with dew, and my locks with the drops of the night' (AV).

> Were all my loud, evil days
> Calm and unhaunted as is thy dark Tent
> ... Then I in Heaven all the long year
> Would keep, and never wander here.

The night is made the equivalent of heaven, because of its sense of peace. It reminds us of Vaughan's own poem, 'Peace'. Vaughan has a tremendous nostalgia for the peace that comes from being in the natural world. We remember that he was writing during the Civil War:

> But living where the sun
> Doth all things wake, and where all mix and tire
> Themselves and others ...

There are definitely two worlds described here. The one is the world with its crazy amount of busy activity, which the worldly sun is partly responsible for, and we think of Donne's 'busy, old fool, unruly sun' in his poem 'The Sun Rising'. This is the world which leads us into all sorts of unnecessary problems, the 'mire', as Vaughan puts it, and there there is heaven which is the abode of peace. And so we lead up to the wonderful climax of this poem, which is surprising in its quiet refusal to be triumphalist:

> There is in God (some say)
> A deep, but dazzling darkness; as men here
> Say it is late and dusky, because they
> See not all clear ...

Paradox is writ large. How can we possibly have a dazzling darkness? The paradox comes about because we are dealing with two worlds, or realities, and the reality of one is perceived by the other only through its opposite. Because we cannot conceive of the brightness of the light of God (as in Dionysius), we do better to describe it by its opposite, than miss, by describing it as less than it really is. It is a daring thing to do, to describe God. Vaughan to a certain extent hides behind Dionysius in doing so; 'some say' we assume is Dionysius, but he gives a homely example to help us out. Some people who don't see too clearly say, 'it's getting dark'. The blindness is in their own eyes,

123

not in the external reality. And so we talk of God being a darkness, because that is the way we perceive it, conscious that it is because we live in another reality, different from God. That reality, our reality, is the world.

> O for that night! where I in him
> Might live invisible and dim.

We accept our little story about bad eyesight, and we perceive God as night because of our own limited human standpoint. Then, knowing that the earthly night itself has such riches and benefits which Christ knew, and Vaughan himself longed for, he finishes the poem with a fine couplet, longing, really, for the quiet, hidden, and retired life which God can offer through 'hid Divinity'.

Interlude

At the Grave of Henry Vaughan

Above the voiceful windings of a river
An old green slab of simply graven stone
Shuns notice, overshadowed by a yew.
Here Vaughan lies dead, whose name flows on for ever
Through pastures of the spirit washed with dew
And starlit with eternities unknown.

Here sleeps the Silurist; the loved physician;
The face that left no portraiture behind;
The skull that housed white angels and had vision
Of daybreak through the gateways of the mind.
   Here faith and mercy, wisdom and humility
   (Whose influence shall prevail for evermore)
   Shine. And this lowly grave tells Heaven's tranquillity.
   And here stand I, a suppliant at the door.

Siegfried Sassoon
from *The Heart's Journey*, XXV (1929)

125

Editions

The edition of Henry Vaughan's poems which I have used here is
Henry Vaughan, *The Complete Poems*, ed. Rudrum, A., Penguin
Books, 1976.

References

de la Mare, W., originally published as an article in The Times
Literary Supplement, July 15, 1915. Collected in *Private View*.
Faber and Faber Limited, London, 1953, p. 154.

Pseudo-Dionysius, *The Complete Works*. Classics of Western Spirituality, SPCK, London, 1987, p. 263.

Vaughan, H., *The Complete Poems*. Ed. Rudrum, A., Penguin, Harmondsworth, 1976, p. 142.

Vaughan, *Complete Poems*, pp. 63–64.

5

THOMAS TRAHERNE
1636–74

For meditative and devotional reading (a little bit at a time, more like sucking a lozenge than eating a slice of bread) I suggest the *Imitation of Christ* (astringent), and Traherne's *Centuries* (joyous).

> C. S. Lewis, letter
> (Source unknown)

There are varieties of gifts, but the same Spirit ... One, through the Spirit, has the gift of wise speech, while another, by the power of the same Spirit, can put the deepest knowledge into words.

> 1 Corinthians 12.4, 8

to speak fully and distinctly
   concerning love

> Thomas Traherne (MS 1360, fol. 126r)

Thomas Traherne was born in Hereford in 1636. He was the son of a shoemaker, but we are not to assume that he was born into poverty. A shoemaker, at the time, was a significant job, and Traherne's father would have had two apprentices working under him, and would have been a respected member of a guild. So almost from the beginning there is something of a contradiction between the assumed biographical stance of his writing, and the historical life. 'Once I remember, I think I was about four years old, when I thus reasoned with myself, sitting in a little obscure room in my father's poor house, If there be a God, certainly he must be infinite in goodness' (*Centuries* 3.16).

Traherne's parents seem to have died when he was young. He was six in 1642 when the Civil War started. Battles raged around Hereford, a garrison town, which changed hands three times in the course of the war. In 1653 when he was 17 he became a student at Brasenose College, Oxford, taking his BA degree in 1656.

It was in pursuit of happiness, he tells us, that he returned to Herefordshire in 1657. 'When I came into the country, and being seated among silent trees, had all my time in my own hands, I resolved to spend it all, whatever it cost me in search of happiness' (*Centuries* 3.46). He was appointed by Puritans under the Commonwealth as Rector of the parish of Credenhill, four miles north-west of Hereford. When the Interregnum ended in 1660, and on the restoration of the monarchy and of the episcopal order in the Church of England, Traherne was ordained and reappointed to Credenhill. He remained rector until he died in 1674.

Some time towards the end of the 1660s he became a private chaplain to Sir Orlando Bridgman, a prominent figure at the court of Charles II, and it was at his house at Teddington that Traherne died in the autumn of 1674, at the age of 38. During his lifetime he published one book, *Roman Forgeries*, 1673. The year after his death his *Christian Ethicks, the Way to Blessedness* appeared, in which, writing 'Of the Nature of Felicity', he produced something of an epitaph: 'The more honour and pleasure we enjoy, the greater and more perfect is our present happiness; though many times in the way to felicity we are forced to quit all these, for the preservation of our innocence.' There we see something of the pull between London and Hereford, the chaplaincy in Teddington and the country priest in Credenhill. With the publication of *Christian Ethicks* the story of Thomas Traherne might have ended for ever: a name, with two books to his credit, in the card index of the British Library.

I do not think that anyone seriously reading Thomas Traherne could fail to enjoy the experience. I know that is a large claim, and difficult to verify, but it comes from the knowledge that Traherne himself set out to share this one burning reality he felt, which was his joy, and the experience of many who read his works is one of the joy that he communicates. 'Enjoy' and 'serious' are strange words to put together, but in a way they fit with Traherne's great contribution to religious writing, and more specifically, Christian mysticism, and that is the profound sense of 'joy' that lies at the heart of a faith in God. There is also something about his enthusiasm, and both his love for God and God's love for him, that conveys itself in his prose style. His subject and his style are one. In terms of his writing, mercy

129

and peace have met together. There is also an enormous energy
in his writing. It is certainly not squeezed out, but like a brilli-
ant cricketer, century follows century. In his writing there is
always an abundance of the same, and at the heart of it there
is a vision which directs the whole. That vision is the vision of
Adam in the garden at the dawn of the world: 'certainly Adam
in Paradise had not more sweet and curious apprehensions of
the world, than I when I was a child' (*Centuries* 3.1). If you can
imagine, and enter sympathetically into that sort of vision,
then you will have no trouble with the worldview of Thomas
Traherne.

Some people are natural inhabitants of Eden before the fall,
but they are few. They are rare in more ways than one, because
they are the people who see the glory in all things with a childlike enthusiasm which is new and fresh. They are people who
might have experienced all sorts of tragedy in their lives, and
have been beset by all manner of illness and struggle, and yet
are continually seeing the good side of things, finding the glory
in the smallest details of the natural world. They are patient
with human vagaries, and they shine with the freshness of the
newly risen sun. They have all the childlike freedom of exag-
geration and surprise. They hang light to law and are full of
grace. When we say about professionals they are 'naturals', in
this case, we could say Traherne was a 'natural' with God.

As so often, it is a matter of how you see things. We could go
into the deep psychological reasons as to why Traherne saw the
world as he did. If we read the works without any biographical
knowledge, we could be forgiven for not knowing that Traherne lived through the Civil War, except for a couple of
passages in an increasingly large body of writing. People
around Traherne were dying of wounds and plague. He died
himself at the age of 37. He shared with so many others the
acute sense of disruption in his Christian ministry, through the
actions of the Parliament period. This sense, of Traherne
writing oblivious of his times, could be maddening, were it not
for the fact that his vision touches a deep chord within us, which
senses that everything that is, is made by God: 'All appeared
new and strange at the first, inexpressibly rare and delightful
and beautiful.' Perhaps Traherne saw through the veneer of
outward circumstances, and was always touching the deep

intentions of God which were longing to come to the surface, and in time would. Love gives a new perspective to the eye – if we see the world with the heart and eye of God.

Traherne's *Centuries of Meditations* contains five books, each of a hundred short passages of meditative writings, except for the fifth which has only ten sections. One of the best-known passages, which has been set to music by Gerald Finzi under the title *Dies Natalis*, is the description of a transfigured landscape of a field of wheat. I deal with this section in the examples, at the end of this chapter. There are many other passages which describe that same sense of the transfiguration of the natural world by the Spirit: the Spirit which kindled the vision of Traherne, and awakened for him the glory in all things:

> All appeared new and strange at the first, inexpressibly rare and delightful and beautiful. I was a little stranger which at my entrance into the world was saluted and surrounded with innumerable joys. My knowledge was divine. I knew by intuition those things which since my apostasy I collected again by the highest reason. My very ignorance was advantageous. I seemed as one brought into the estate of innocence. All things were spotless and pure and glorious: yea infinitely mine, and joyful and precious. I knew not that there were any sins, or complaints or laws. I dreamed not of poverties, contentions or vices. All tears and quarrels were hidden from mine eyes. Everything was at rest, free and immortal. I was entertained like an angel with the works of God in their splendour and glory. I saw all in the peace of Eden. Heaven and Earth did sing my Creator's praises, and could not make more melody to Adam, than to me. (*Centuries* 3.2)

The phenomenon that is Traherne is surrounded, not only for me but for all those who know anything about him, with serendipity, miracle, providence, with 'profitable wonders'. How the twentieth century came to rediscover Traherne, is a fairy tale in its own right. Someone was rummaging round in a barrow of secondhand books in London, in 1896, and came across a manuscript which was first thought to be by Henry Vaughan. On closer inspection, it turned out to be the work of Thomas Traherne. In 1967, his *Commentaries of Heaven*, another manuscript, was rescued from a bonfire in Wigan, by a man looking for spare parts for a car, and just recently, in 1997, another hidden work, *The Kingdom of Heaven*, has been recognized as by Traherne; this time it was found on the shelves of the Lambeth Palace Library. With the enthusiastic research that is going on at the moment, we will know much more about the life of this poet, writer, and priest, and of one who saw into the heart of things.

The chance wonder with which the last century rediscovered Traherne's writings is echoed in my own schoolboy experience. I came across a book in the library of a Franciscan monastery in Worcestershire. Worcester is not so far from Credenhill in Herefordshire, where Traherne was the parish priest. I did not know that then. I knew nothing of the writer of the book that I had picked off the library shelves. The monastery is set on a rise, and has a view to the west across to the Abberley hills. Why I should pick that book to take out early in the morning, and why I should open it at the page which begins 'The corn was orient and immortal wheat' I shall never know, but that was the case, and it was a case of the word speaking directly to me with tremendous power and resonance.

We know comparatively little about Traherne's life, but we do get a very clear picture of his religious mind. One important fact about his thought is that it circles round an extremely strong sense of the glory of childhood. Two quotations from Scripture come immediately to mind: 'Whoever does not accept the Kingdom of God like a child will never enter it', and 'out of the mouths of babes and sucklings'. Childhood, or children, for Jesus held a secret which adults would do well to relearn. What that secret was, as Jesus saw it, is not quite clear. Was it their innocence, was it their need for affection, or was it the freshness of their view of the world? We shall never know for sure, but 'is it not strange', says Traherne of himself, 'is it not strange, that an infant should be heir of the whole world, and see those mysteries which the books of the learned never unfold.'

There is some discussion as to whether Traherne was really talking about himself or talking out of his own experience about an ideal state of childhood. Or was he imagining how Christ might have understood the nature of childhood innocence? One way or another, for Traherne, childhood held the secret of the angelical life.

What about ourselves and our first 'intimations of immortal-

132

ity', as Wordsworth put it? I don't call on Wordsworth randomly here. There is a strong, spiritual kinship between the writings of Traherne and Wordsworth, but, alas, as yet there is no evidence that Wordsworth read the writings of Traherne. Wordsworth, however, did write a sonnet about a place within a stone's throw of Traherne's Credenhill. He must have known the area quite well: no. 20 of *Miscellaneous Sonnets* is 'Roman Antiquities discovered at Bishopstone, Herefordshire'. Added to that are two other interesting poems by Wordsworth which connect closely with Herefordshire and the seventeenth-century Caroline Divines. One is a poem on St Catherine of Ledbury – Ledbury, again, very near Credenhill – and the other is 'Walton's Book of Lives'. This latter deserves quoting in full, for its perceptive sympathy with all our writers here:

> There are no colours in the fairest sky
> So fair as these. The feather, whence the pen
> Was shaped that traced the lives of these good men,
> Dropped from an angel's wing. With moistened eye
> We read of faith and perfect charity
> In statesman, priest, and humble citizen:
> Oh could we copy their mild virtues, then
> What joy to live, what blessedness to die!
> Methinks their very names shine still and bright;
> Apart – like glow-worms on a summer night;
> Or lonely tapers when from far they fling
> A guiding ray; or seen – like stars on high,
> Satellites burning in a lucid ring
> Around meek Walton's heavenly memory.
>
> *Ecclesiastical Sonnets* 5

Separate, though, from Wordsworth, how do we remember the experiences of our childhood and youth, in relation to God? Did we pick up a shell on the beach, or a twig, or a stone, and hold it as precious? Samuel Beckett, the playwright, said he picked up stones because he felt they were particular for him, as if they were longing for him to pick them up. Did we marvel at the first sight of the sea on our holidays? 'Exultation', wrote Emily Dickinson, 'is the going of an inland soul to sea.' Were we at some time overcome by the awe surrounding the presence of

God in church, or at our prayers, or in the face of another, or in the wonders of natural beauty? Our cynical generation has punched that almost entirely out of us. The generation Traherne lived in was also brutal, but he remembers how he 'was entertained like an angel with the works of God in their splendour and glory. I saw all in the peace of Eden; heaven and earth did sing my creator's praises, and could not make more melody to Adam, than to me' (*Centuries* 3.2).

Something must have happened to Traherne to help him see as he did, so deeply, and with profound faith in the real presence of God existing in all things. There must have been some great movement of the Holy Spirit in his life to allow him to enter into the heart of God where all is hope and light. He must have been aware of all the brutality, crime, and poverty of his own day, and was not blind and uncaring towards that. The churchwarden's account of the parish in the time of Traherne recounts that he visited the sick and the poor of the parish. It is just that he must have been continually aware, beneath all that was transitory, of the abiding sense of the eternal glory of God. Traherne saw things and people, looked under the surface, and deeply into them, so that he could see them, as their destiny might so easily transform them. He saw them as God saw them.

How then did he see the hard and painful things of God's world? How did he understand the crucifixion, for example?

The cross is the abyss of wonders, the centre of desires, the school of virtues, the house of wisdom, the throne of love, the theatre of joys, and the place of sorrows. It is the root of happiness and the gate of heaven. The cross is the most exalted of all objects. It is an ensign lifted up for all the nations, to it shall the Gentiles seek. His rest shall be glorious, the dispersed of Judah shall be gathered together to it, from the four corners of the earth. If love be the weight of the soul, and its object the centre, all eyes and hearts may convert and turn unto this object, cleave unto this centre and by it enter into rest. There we might see all nations assembled with their eyes and hearts upon it. There we may see God's goodness, wisdom and power, yea, his mercy and anger displayed. There we may see man's sin and his infinite value. There we

134

might see the rock of ages and the joys of heaven. There we may see a man loving all the world and a God dying for mankind. (*Centuries* 1, 58, 59)

As with St John's Gospel, you feel, as you read this passage, that God's victory is won from the beginning, and that God has won the victory from the start, because his very being is victorious. There is suffering, Jesus cries out 'I thirst', but it is a willed suffering on behalf of the world, so that the victory and the love of God could be made more visible. Once you have seen and known the love of God, the cross becomes the key to that. Death is swallowed up in victory.

I may have given the impression, through a lack of any description of the context in which Traherne wrote, that this all fell into his lap as if from heaven. Indeed, there is a very strong sense of his being inspired, given gifts of seeing and writing far beyond the ordinary, but two things helped considerably in the production of his writing. One was the encouragement of his friends and fellow writers, who provided a devotional community near Credenhill. Susannah Hopton seems to have been the instigator of this group, and it is possible that the encouragement to write, and disseminate that writing more widely, came from her.

Secondly, Traherne wrote out of a long tradition of mystical writing in the Church. Not all of these writers were orthodox Christians. Plotinus (205–70), Hermes, 'the Thrice-Greatest' (writings are attributed to him from the first to third centuries), Meister Eckhart (1260–1328), and Giordano Bruno (seventeenth century) are in the list, which probably accounts for one lady, who, when I read the works of Traherne to her, said, 'He would probably be called a "new-ager" if he were alive today!'

Among the Church Fathers who Traherne was much influenced by are St Augustine, and more especially, St Gregory Nazianzus (329–89). St Gregory's writings, particularly the *Five Theological Orations* with its elaborate treatment of the Holy Spirit, was a major influence on Traherne. This passage from Gregory, for example, seems very close to Traherne in spirit:

Who gave you the ability to contemplate the beauty of the skies, the course of the sun, the round moon, the millions of stars, the harmony and rhythm that issue from the world as from a lyre, the return of the seasons, the alternation of the months, the demarcation of day and night, the fruits of the earth, the vastness of the air, the ceaseless motion of the waves, the sound of the wind? Who gave you the rain, the soil to cultivate, food to eat, arts, houses, laws, a republic, cultivated manners, friendship with your fellows? (Gregory Nazianzen, in Clement, 1993).

The biblical books are much quoted from, and the 1611 translation of the Bible, with its sonorous and lyrical prose, was close to Traherne's heart. Writers rarely write unaccompanied. Influences stream in, and encouragement, and inspiration from all ages; so what seem original thoughts are often ancient thoughts new-minted. With Traherne, certainly, these individuals and traditions lie behind him, but a combination of these, and a strong personal inspiration, and the strength and beauty of the English language which he used so expansively, all combined to produce Traherne's magnificent genius. No amount of explaining away by sources can account for the lifting of the heart that so often accompanies the reading of his work. That is the gift of Traherne's inspired genius.

Examples

DIARY on 'My Spirit'

'My Spirit' is a poem by Traherne divided into seven verses or sections. When I was reading it, I was reading, at the same time, the account of the creation in Genesis 1, and not surprisingly realized that both were crafted, literary pieces divided into seven sections. Would there be anything to gain by keeping them both in mind at once? And if it is not too difficult, to take the advice of Arthur Clements in his book *The Mystical Poetry of Thomas Traherne* (1969) and have open the prologue to St John's Gospel, and the *Commentary on the Gospel of St John*, by Meister Eckhart. We are into beginnings here, and basics, and roots; into light, and created wonders, and the response of human beings to all of this. We are encouraged to see how we, and God, relate in wonder, and how things far and near, through the glory of God becoming human, are in relationship.

One other footnote to 'My Spirit' is that a series of *Poems from Meditations on the Six Days of the Creation* are part of the *Poetical Works of Thomas Traherne*, edited by Gladys Wade, in 1932. They are now thought to be by Mrs Susanna Hopton, the lady who I referred to earlier as living near to Credenhill, and being of encouragement to Traherne. Meditations on the days of creation were obviously part of the practice of the time, and Traherne, in his own way, in the poem 'My Spirit', is doing his meditation on creation.

DAY ONE – Verse One

My naked simple life was I.
　　　That act so strongly shined
Upon the earth, the sea, the sky,
That was the substance of my mind.
　　　The sense itself was I.
I felt no dross nor matter in my soul,
No brims nor borders, such as in a bowl
We see, my essence was capacity.
　　　　　That felt all things
　　　　　he thought that springs

137

Therefrom's itself. It hath no other wings
To spread abroad, nor eyes to see,
Nor hands distinct to feel,
Nor knees to kneel:
But being simple like the Deity
In its own centre is a sphere
Not shut up here, but everywhere.

In response to Moses' question in Exodus, 'Who shall I say sent me?', God replies 'I AM that I am. Tell them that "I AM" has sent you to them' (Exodus 3.14). God gives away a mysterious, but also deeply revealing name. The name says that God is the very essence of being itself. In the Genesis account of creation, it is God who gives being and existence to the world, out of his own will and desire. When Traherne reflects on his own beginnings and looks back, he writes, 'My naked simple life was I.' Traherne describes himself in the same way that God describes himself to Moses, 'I am that I am'. I am bound up in the totality of my being. 'My naked, simple', childlike being describes the state of a child, who, more than adults, lives very much in the world of its own experience. By that simplicity and total inwardness children experience a total outwardness as well. Traherne, in his childlike existence, is what he is, with no duplicity, no acting, nothing hidden or crafted, and no sin. Traherne is here, perhaps (and there will be quite a few 'perhapses') thinking not so much of a physical beginning, as a spiritual beginning. That sort of spiritual beginning is similar to the moment of a conversion, a new birth, when, at one moment, everything seems to come together. At a time in history, during and after the Civil War, when everything was falling apart, and violence and hatred were experienced all around, a new vision comes to lead Traherne to the way things are meant to be. It is only glimpsed by this gift of seeing, through the dark to the original light.

DAY TWO – Verse Two

It acts not from a centre to
Its object as remote,
But present is, when it doth view
Being with the being it doth note.

138

Whatever it doth do,
It doth not by another engine work,
But by itself; which in the act doth lurk.
Its essence is transformed into a true
And perfect act.
And so exact
Hath God appeared in this mysterious fact,
That 'tis all eye, all act, all sight,
And what it please can be,
Not only see,
Or do; for 'tis more voluble than light:
Which can put on ten thousand forms,
Being clothed with what itself adorns.

What is 'It'? 'It', is the Spirit, as in the title, 'My Spirit'. It is his own Spirit of which he is writing. Holding on to that fact is very important, now we are on the rock face with few tangible footholds. We are dealing here with the Spirit, and the Spirit defies easy definition. It is not something that can be easily measured. Scientists have got the wind measured, gale force, light breeze, and so on, but the Spirit, which is much like the wind in other respects, in respect of definition, remains elusive. The Spirit, 'My Spirit' also has no definable boundaries. We are no longer on the rock face. We are in free fall. The barriers are breaking down between being and doing, and between the looker and the looked at.

DAY THREE – Verse Three

This made me present evermore
With whatsoe'er I saw,
An object if it were before
My eye, was by Dame Nature's law,
Within my soul. Her store
Was all at once within me; all her treasures
Were my immediate and internal pleasures,
Substantial joys, which did inform my mind.
With all she wrought
My soul was fraught,
And every object in my soul a thought
Begot, or was; I could not tell,

139

> Whether the things did there
> Themselves appear,
> Which in my spirit truly seemed to dwell;
> Or whether my conforming mind
> Were not alone even all that shined.

No boundaries, but a connecting influence: the Spirit is a go-between God which links the eye with the object seen, the being with the doing, the 'essence' with the 'act':

> This made me present evermore
> With whatso'er I saw.

We say sometimes we become what we eat, but that is equally true of what we see. If we look long enough on evil, we shall be influenced by it, which is why we are cautious, would we were more so, by the exposure of children to images of evil.

Similarly, the more we gaze on God, and on the true, and the beautiful, the more we will be affected by them.

> Her store
> Was all at once within me; all her treasures
> Were my immediate and internal pleasures . . .

How different we feel when we get out into the open country-side, or even into our gardens, or stand beside the sea, or climb a hill or a mountain. How much better we can feel when we are in the presence of a good person, a saint, who casts a benign influence, an aura of peace and goodness, around themselves, and on us, and we can just share in that and feel better.

DAY FOUR – Verse Four

> But yet of this I was most sure,
> That at the utmost length,
> (So worthy was it to endure)
> My soul could best express its strength.
> It was so quick and pure,
> That all my mind was wholly everywhere
> What e'er it saw, 'twas ever wholly there;
> The sun ten thousand legions off, was nigh:
> The utmost star
> Tho' seen from far,

140

Was present in the apple of my eye.
There was my sight, my life, my sense,
My substance and my mind
My spirit shined
Even there, not by a transient influence.
The act was immanent, yet there.
The thing remote, yet felt even here.

'My ... my ... my ...': that could be very self-absorbed, self-concerned, but Traherne's 'my' quite naturally becomes my own personal pronoun. Traherne's personal vision, spoken personally, gets easily shared, and becomes our vision, our concern. Soul and mind get a bit tangled here, and so do all the other senses, and the organized ideas of near and far. Something is going on which brings everything so much together, and yet does not, like colours when all mixed together, turn into a brown mess. Things are one, and yet maintain their particularity, and all things are working together for good. It is a vision with no evil, no darkness, those things have been banished from the scene. We are back before the Garden of Eden, at the dawn of the creation of the sun and the stars, where everything is both good and gift:

The utmost star
Tho' seen from far,
Was present in the apple of my eye.

DAY FIVE – Verse Five

O joy! O wonder, and delight!
O sacred mystery!
My soul a spirit infinite!
An image of the Deity!
A pure substantial light!
That being greatest which doth nothing seem!
Why 'twas my all, I nothing did esteem
But that alone. A strange mysterious sphere!
A deep abyss
That sees and is
The only proper place or bower of bliss.
To its Creator 'tis so near

In love and excellence
In life and sense,
In greatness, worth and nature; and so dear;
In it, without hyperbole,
The Son and friend of God we see.

It would have been neat if this verse had been number six, and
then the creation of human beings would have coincided with
the reference to the glory of the creation, of 'an image of the
Deity'. Nevertheless, here is the verse which marvels and revels
in the miracle of humanity. You wake up of a morning, and
realize just how remarkable being alive is, and discover the privilege of being human. This is 'What a piece of work is man!'
without Hamlet's pessimistic ending. The rejoicing and thanksgiving are maintained for the gift of being human, being alive,
and being 'the Son and friend of God'. The obvious echo in this
last line takes us in our thoughts to Jesus, who both shared our
humanity, and brought creation, potentially, back to its original
shine for us.

DAY SIX – Verse Six

A strange extended orb of joy,
Proceeding from within,
Which did on every side convey
Itself, and being nigh of kin
To God did every way
Dilate itself even in an instant, and
Like an indivisible centre stand
At once surrounding all eternity.
'Twas not a sphere
Yet did appear
One infinite. 'Twas somewhat everywhere.
And tho' it had a power to see
Far more, yet still it shined
And was a mind
Exerted for it saw infinity
'Twas not a sphere, but 'twas a power
Invisible, and yet a bower.

What is at one moment the centre is, the next, surrounding
everything. This is a paradox, a strange contradictory thing,

reflecting the impossibility of knowing God in simple, human terms or words. God always defies our definitions. He is the Jack-in-the-box, now Jack, now the box, and now both Jack and the box at the same time. This is God's prerogative.

> Like an indivisible centre stand
> At once surrounding all eternity

and again:

> 'Twas somewhat everywhere.

God's Spirit which sees fit to enter our spirit is utterly without boundaries, and what better image for that than light. God said, 'Let there be light', and in John's prologue, 'He was the light of the world', and Meister Eckhart commenting on this prologue writes:

> And light shines in darkness, as though to say; in the case of created things nothing shines, nothing is known, nothing effects knowledge, save the quiddity, the essential nature, of the thing itself, its definition or idea.

> . . . yet still it shined
> And was a mind
> Exerted for it saw infinity.

Notice Eckhart's 'nothing shines', and Traherne's 'still it shined'. The light shines in, and through, the darkness. The idea, at the very heart of our motivation, shines out. C. S. Lewis was worried about Traherne's lack of a sense of the presence of evil, and I can understand that. The idea under discussion in the poem might be an evil one, and then would it shine? Traherne takes it for granted that the idea comes from a vision of God, and therefore it naturally reflects the goodness of God. So there is a huge importance, and responsibility, on where our eyes are fixed. Our eyes are fixed where true joys are to be found, on God alone.

DAY SEVEN – Verse Seven

> O wondrous self! O sphere of light,
>   O sphere of joy most fair;
> O act, O power infinite;
> O subtle, and unbounded air!

O living orb of sight!
Thou which within me art, yet me! Thou eye,
And temple of his whole infinity!
O what a world art thou! a world within!
All things appear
All objects are
Alive in thee! Supersubstantial, rare
Above themselves, and nigh of kin
To those pure things we find
In his great mind
Who made the world! tho' now eclipsed by sin.
There they are useful and divine.
Exalted there they ought to shine.

By the end of the poem I begin to recognize familiar words, or clusters of words. I begin to notice 'shine' around which clusters 'eye' and 'light'. 'Sphere' gathers 'centre' round it in conjunction with it, and also in contrast to it, and 'orb' finds its place here too. Instead of detailing practical, tangible things, Traherne works with states of being, and with the continual clash of opposites, from which shines truth, which has to be sensed rather than understood.

Where are we left at the end of this poem? I feel on the edge of a new and different world. What I see is a galaxy, and the contemporary image might be one of travelling in space. I see spheres and orbs through the cockpit window, and sense a feeling of weightlessness, disorientation, and the sheer size of the area in which Traherne's imagination is working. It is like looking at a huge working model of the universe and then remembering that I am standing in it, and am a part of it, and finally realizing that it is in my heart, as close to me as that, and it is glorious, and the glory shines in, and the glory shines out.

'*The corn* was orient and immortal wheat'

Will you see the infancy of this sublime and celestial greatness? I was a stranger, which at my entrance into the world was saluted and surrounded with innumerable joys; my knowledge was divine. I was entertained like an angel with the works of God in their splendour and glory. Heaven and

144

earth did sing my Creator's praises and could not make more melody to Adam than to me. Certainly Adam in Paradise had not more sweet and curious apprehensions of the world than I. All appeared new, and strange at first, inexpressibly rare and delightful and beautiful. All things were spotless and pure and glorious. The corn was orient and immortal wheat, which never should be reaped nor was ever sown. I thought it had stood from everlasting to everlasting. The green trees, when I saw them first, transported and ravished me, their sweetness and their unusual beauty made my heart to leap, and almost mad with ecstacy, they were such strange and wonderful things. O what venerable creatures did the aged seem! Immortal cherubims! And the young men glittering and sparkling angels, and maids strange seraphic pieces of life and beauty! I knew not that they were born or should die but all things abided eternally. I knew not that there were sins or complaints or laws. I dreamed not of poverties, contentions or vices. All tears and quarrels were hidden from my eyes. I saw all in the peace of Eden. Everything was at rest, free and immortal.

This piece comes from the *Centuries of Meditations*, 3.1,2 and 3. I have used this version because it has been set to music by Gerald Finzi (1901–56) in a work called *Dies Natalis*, cantata for high voice and strings, opus 8, and it is one of those settings that seems to have captured completely the essence of Traherne's writings. The passage works well without the music, and for the complete text you would need to get hold of *Centuries of Meditations* by Thomas Traherne, in an edition which you can find listed at the end of the chapter.

I suppose that this piece could be taken on a purely emotional level. There are a lot of phrases in it to help us with that: 'sweet apprehensions', new things 'inexpressibly rare and delightful and beautiful', the trees transporting and ravishing, 'made my heart to leap and almost mad with ecstacy'. Yet, although the internal emotions of Traherne are all well described, there is also an external world which is fairly clearly painted in: corn, trees, the elderly, young men, and maids. We have the familiar territory of a person experiencing the outside world, of any time or place.

145

It is also a strange and unusual world, because it has been transfigured through the eyes of the one looking out at it. Experiences of transfiguration, when the landscape, or a person, take on a new and glorious form in our eyes, are not uncommon. They can be experienced when the light of the day has a magical glow, or you feel yourself particularly happy. You are in love, you have passed an exam, you have overcome a difficulty, you have been forgiven your sins. Both you and the world seem transformed, for the better.

What the cause of Traherne's joy was, is more difficult to understand. It seems to be concerned with beginnings, and Adam in the Garden of Eden has an important part to play in the description, even if only as a contrast to the extent of Traherne's joy. 'Certainly Adam in Paradise had not more sweet and curious apprehensions of the world than I.' It is a state before sin and failure have made their mark. 'My knowledge was divine.' The cause seems to have been something to do with a close relationship with God, so close that Traherne could say his 'knowledge was divine'. He looked out with the eyes of God, and in that sense, we could say he was partaking of the divine nature. He had put on the mind of Christ, as St Paul commended. The joy came from outside himself. 'I was a stranger, which at my entrance into the world was saluted and surrounded with innumerable joys.'

We could say Traherne had arrived in heaven, but we feel it is a heaven on earth. The familiar is still around, but it has changed. The young are 'glittering and sparkling angels'. Traherne had entered the eternal dimension. It was a glimpse of glory, it was what it might be like ... 'if only'. The vision certainly bears the hallmark of a conversion, of an embrace by God, a transforming kiss of peace, a step out of doubt and despair into belief.

All is transformed, because the heart is transformed. We looked out on corn, and the grains have grown into full-blown wheat, shining in the summer sun with an orient glow. In the seventeenth century they used to talk about a special kind of wheat which was called holy wheat, or summer wheat, and a traveller in 1632 wrote 'I found the wheat here growing higher than my head.' This wheat of Traherne's is 'orient and immortal wheat, which never should be reaped nor was ever sown'. It

146

is remarkable how moving this particular line is. Partly it is to do with the bold juxtaposition of something so ordinary, usual, day-to-day, with the idea of wheat being divine, immortal, a symbol of the Godhead. And yet that is not unusual, and a bell rings in our minds, and we remember the bread of the Holy Communion, which becomes, in a mystical way, the immortal Body of Christ. The corn becomes immortal wheat, and the bread becomes the Body of Christ. In that short sentence so many levels of meaning are packed in. Not to mention our experience, on a more worldly level, of the sight of a field of wheat stroked by the sun on a summer's evening, with a slight breeze swaying the cloth-of-gold, in a great unison sway.

This passage of the *Centuries* describes Traherne's return to innocence, or his paradise regained. What is regained is the childhood which was guileless and uncritical, lacking in judgement, open to influence. Can we just about remember it? And how much it depended on the love and warmth of those who were looking after us.

I do not really want to finish on a critical note, but what is this saying to those who have been brutalized as children, abused, forgotten, neglected, hated? I feel that it is an offering of hope, and a challenge. The hope it offers is that God has given us humanity, the opportunity to be fully human and to live at peace with joy and fulfilment, but we have gone astray from that vision, and the faults are cumulative. Heroic efforts have been made, and are being made, to reverse the faults and disasters, and if there was not some vision to work towards, then there would be no hope at all, but there is hope. Traherne holds out a picture of hope.

The challenge is to find ways of entering into the inheritance of glory, to rediscover the glory that is ours, and the health of the planet. We need to learn about it, and to be taught how to use it and to claim it as stewards of creation. Traherne may be considered unrealistic, too optimistic, no earthly use, but his joy is catching, and it touches deep chords within people. We have journeyed too far from our essential blessedness, our inherent goodness in God, but given a sense of purpose we can be drawn back to the same blessed state, be it in heaven or on earth.

'I knew not that there were sins or complaints or laws.' Be

realistic, Traherne! But what did Jesus come to do, but be a means of forgiving sins, of showing us the power of grace and love over law, and of his dying on the cross, as he redeemed the world. There may be a long way for us to go to be Christ-like, but that is no excuse for not starting, and starting with the hope of success that Traherne gives us. Some people see further and deeper than others, and are given the gift of putting the deepest things into words. It is a gift of the Spirit, and as we read Traherne, we feel sure we are in the presence of one who was given that spiritual gift.

Editions

PROSE

Centuries of Meditations was first published in 1908 by the editor Bertram Dobell. This edition is still available from second-hand bookshops. Selections have been published, most recently that edited by Allchin, A. M., *Landscapes of Glory*, Darton Longman and Todd, London, 1989.

POETRY

The poems of Traherne were first published in 1903, with a second edition in 1906. These editions are rare. The third edition, with addition of *Poems of Felicity*, was published in 1932, by P. J. and A. E. Dobell, with the title, *The Poetical Works of Thomas Traherne*, edited with preface and notes by Gladys I. Wade.

References

Eckhart, M., *Selected Treatises and Summaries*. Ed. Clark, J. M. and Skinner, J. V., Faber and Faber Limited, London, 1958, p. 236.

Gregory Nazianzen, *On Love for the Poor, 23*. Quoted in Clement, O., *The Roots of Christian Mysticism*. New City, London, 1993, p. 17.

Griffin, W., *C. S. Lewis, The Authentic Voice*. Lion Publishing, Oxford, 1988.

MS 1360 (fol. 126r), Lambeth Palace Library.

The Society for Promoting Christian Knowledge (SPCK) was founded in 1698. Its mission statement is:

To promote Christian knowledge by

- **Communicating the Christian faith in its rich diversity**
- **Helping people to understand the Christian faith and to develop their personal faith; and**
- **Equipping Christians for mission and ministry**

SPCK Worldwide serves the Church through Christian literature and communication projects in 100 countries, and provides books for those training for ministry in many parts of the developing world. This worldwide service depends upon the generosity of others and all gifts are spent wholly on ministry programmes, without deductions.

SPCK Bookshops support the life of the Christian community by making available a full range of Christian literature and other resources, providing support for those training for ministry, and assisting bookstalls and book agents throughout the UK.

SPCK Publishing produces Christian books and resources, covering a wide range of inspirational, pastoral, practical and academic subjects. Authors are drawn from many different Christian traditions, and publications aim to meet the needs of a wide variety of readers in the UK and throughout the world.

The Society does not necessarily endorse the individual views contained in its publications, but hopes they stimulate readers to think about and further develop their Christian faith.

For information about the Society, visit our website at *www.spck.org.uk*, or write to:
SPCK, Holy Trinity Church, Marylebone Road,
London NW1 4DU, United Kingdom.